NAMES WILL NEVER HURT ME

HOW TO DEAL WITH PEOPLE WHO MINIMIZE YOU, IGNORE YOU, ABUSE YOU AND BULLY YOU

ANN ANDREWS

ACTIVITY PRESS

TESTIMONIALS

In *Names Will Never Hurt Me*, Ann Andrews covers a difficult subject with a great touch and an optimistic tone. My interest is particularly in the area of workplace bullying, an area that Ann covers with insight and practical actions. The book is very readable. Ann is uniquely qualified to write this book—both because of her unfortunate early life experience and because she has helped many people deal with abuse. The book is highly recommended to anyone who has someone who is deliberately violating their personal power.

Andrew O'Keeffe, author of *The Boss*, *Hardwired Humans* and *First Leaders*

Names Will Never Hurt Me is a compelling book that many people will easily relate to. Research shows that exposure to bullying is linked to long-term adverse mental health consequences, and this book provides good guidance about what it is, and also what it is not. I particularly enjoyed the real-life stories, the clear points to look for, and steps on what we can do if we think we're being bullied. It's so easy to read and follow, and it also provides guidance on how we can implement simple, yet effective measures against bullies.

Orquidea Tamayo Mortera, RDRTh, Programme Lead – Diversional Therapy

Yet again, Ann Andrews puts the human in HR through her mastery of confronting life-changing workplace and real-world topics head-on. Her latest book delves into the psychological and organisational impact that exposure to bullying has on our personal and professional lives. Through her own experiences and wisdom, Ann empowers us to understand ourselves better so we can recognise and positively impact the negative behaviour of others. If awareness is the first step to addressing the bullying crisis and unmasking the bully, reading this book is the right place to start.

Craig Garner, Advocate, consultant and contributor to sustainable values-based business

I've just read Ann's latest book, *Names Will Never Hurt Me*. Yet another work of genius. Arguably her best to date.

Ann has an incredible ability to deal with topics that desperately need dealing with. She always uses plain simple language that gets straight to the point. Her message is never lost in the ephemeral mists of PC babble.

Throughout this latest work she quotes from her personal experiences, talks about how she responded to those experiences and the outcomes of her responses, good and bad. She talks about how to recognise when people are behaving badly towards us, which is something 'every' one of us experiences at least some of the time, and something most of us avoid confronting.

Most importantly, she provides a pathway to a better future. A future largely free of badly behaving others. This book is a must read for everybody. (No exceptions.) It contains the keys to the kingdom of freedom from bad behaviour. It's for you if you know you're treated badly, at least some of the time. It's also for you if you naively believe you're never treated badly by others.

Read the book and enjoy the journey.

Chris Baker, Country Manager, PeopleMaps NZ/Aus

Sadly, bullying has become more visible over the last few years magnified through social media.

Rarely has there been a book that provides such an insight into adult bullying or shared so many stories, resources, and books to help us all to understand and tackle bullying in our lives.

Ann has taken her personal and work experiences and channelled them into this book.

Her 30+ years working in HR helping to create effective teams has given her a rare insight into bullying in the workplace. Her personal experiences added to her recent work with *Women Behaving Courageously* has rounded out her understanding of the issues. This book shares a wealth of ways to tackle bullying in all its guises and recognises that no one solution works for everyone.

This is an invaluable book that we should all read and share both for ourselves if we are or have experienced bullying but also so that we can all understand and identify bullying when we see it happening around us. Awareness and support are key ways for us to tackle such an insidious problem.

Pam Martin, Serial Connector, Judge The David Awards (www.thedavidawards.co.nz)

Copyright © 2024 Ann Andrews

Ann Andrews asserts her moral right to be identified as the author of this work.

All rights reserved. No part of this publication may be produced or transmitted in any form or by any means, electronic or mechanical, including photocopying, recording or information storage and retrieval systems, without permission in writing from the copyright holder.

Published by Activity Press
Contact author: www.annandrews.co.nz

A catalogue record for this book is available from the National Library of New Zealand.

ISBN 978-1-0670212-0-7 (Paperback)
ISBN 978-1-0670212-1-4 (EPUB)

CONTENTS

Introduction   xiii
Warning   xix

How the chapters unfold   1

1. **FIRST BASE: UNDERSTANDING YOURSELF**   5
   Understanding the first 0–7 years of our lives   5
   Our family of origin   7
   Learned behaviours   8
   Limiting beliefs   9
   Place in the family   10
   The era you were born   11
   Fathers and sons   12
   The culture you were born into   13
   When cultures collide   13
   My own 0–7 years   15
   My first women's groups   20
   Ending the patterns that have taken over our lives for better or worse   22

2. **WHY CAN'T PEOPLE BE MORE LIKE ME?**   23
   I'm OK, you're not so hot   23
   Understanding the difference between assertiveness and aggression   29
   Understanding the critical importance of having a healthy self-esteem   30
   A self-esteem test   31

3. **HOW TO ADDRESS INAPPROPRIATE BEHAVIOURS IN YOUR TEAM**   32
   Signs of a toxic work environment   32
   Dealing with conflict in teams   35
   Exercise: The behaviours we do NOT want in this team   37
   Exercise: The behaviours we DO want in this team   37
   Exercise: How to create a set of ground rules   37

Ensuring people abide by the Ground Rules	39
Understanding projection in team members	40

4. **BULLIES AT WORK** — 44
   - When conflict turns into bullying and harassment — 44
   - What bullying ISN'T — 46
   - What bullying IS — 48
   - The confusion between bullying and harassment — 50
   - The difference between a bully and a narcissist — 51
   - Is narcissism on the rise? — 52
   - Is there a positive side to narcissism? — 53
   - Understanding narcissism in management — 54
   - How to deal with a bully if you are their target — 56
   - The effects of bullying — 58
   - Why do people bully others? — 59
   - Effects on the bully — 60
   - Can bullies change their destructive behaviour? — 60
   - Understanding and dealing with sexual harassment — 61
   - Dealing with online bullying — 62

5. **STRATEGIES FOR DEALING WITH BULLYING AT HOME** — 66
   - Delay tactics we fall prey to — 66
   - Naming the Game — 68
   - Exercise: Define what and who — 72
   - Acknowledge the patterns you've allowed to occur — 74
   - Is your significant other a bully? A test. — 75
   - Learning to stand your ground — 78
   - Reactions to you standing your ground — 80
   - Some basic techniques for dealing with reactions — 81
   - The power of hand gestures — 83
   - What to say, when to say it and how to say it — 85
   - Dealing with a tricky work situation — 85
   - Handling a tense family situation — 87
   - Neutral phrases that no one can argue with — 91
   - The *Toughlove* strategy for dealing with conflict — 92
   - Learn to fight fairly — 94
   - Deciding to try a different strategy — 96
   - Deciding to do nothing — 97
   - What not to DO ever — 99
   - What not to SAY ever — 99

Live to fight another day	100
Learn to choose your battles	102
What to do if *their* behaviour slips back	103
What to do if *you* slip back into old habits	104

6. YOUR FUTURE IS COMING READY OR NOT — 109

Learning to forgive	109
What if you 'chose' your parents?	110
Learning to say NO so you have the time and energy to say YES	111
Become your own best friend	113

7. YOU'RE NEVER TOO OLD AND IT'S NEVER TOO LATE — 115

Setting up a future where naysayers, abusers and bullies keep out of your way because they know you no longer play that game	115
Keeping your self-esteem intact now and forever	116
What's your what next?	116
Where would you aim if you knew you couldn't fail?	117
As one door closes, another always opens	118

8. FEEL THE FEAR AND MOVE AHEAD ANYWAY — 122

The journey of 1000 miles starts with a single step	122
Do regular mental/physical/spiritual checks	123
Believe in miracles	124
Know you're supported	125
You've just climbed your mountain	125

9. FURTHER RESOURCES — 127

Great quotes if you ever feel you are slipping back into old victim behaviours	127
My 40-year reading list (alphabetical)	132
Resources if your child is being bullied	135
Counselling Services in New Zealand	136

About the Author	137
Books by the author	139
Acknowledgments	141
Sources	143

This book is dedicated to my courageous granddaughter Tayla who was bullied mercilessly at school and tackled the problem by becoming a black belt in Taekwondo.

Never mess with a young woman who has a black belt in Taekwondo

INTRODUCTION

I'd originally planned to write this book for women: particularly for women who'd been attending my *'Women Behaving Courageously'* live workshops and webinars. I wanted to be able to give them skills and strategies to take home or back to work to have the confidence to deal with totally unacceptable behaviours.

Then I realized men are bullied also. Young men get bullied by older men under the guise of 'teasing'; older men can be bullied by younger more tech-savvy work colleagues and made to feel dumb and inadequate because they're not proficient in technology or are getting a bit slower as they age.

I've even met men who are in straight and gay relationships who've confessed to me that they're bullied by their partners. It can be so easy for the least assertive person in any relationship to become a full-on target of the more assertive person in the couple.

This book then, is for anyone, young or old, male or female, gay or straight who is feeling powerless in the face of someone being abusive to them. It's for people who are in a toxic relationship or are part of a dysfunctional family: it's especially for people who work in a toxic business environment because bullying can happen to anyone, anywhere, any time. It can be verbal, physical or online. It can be obvious or secretive. However it occurs, it is debilitating for the target.

I've written numerous business books over the years; almost all of them focusing on building high-performing teams and on some aspect of business leadership.

I worked with high-performing teams for over 30 years and taught team members how to speak up if they were feeling pressured to do things that didn't sit well with them or if they were the target of inappropriate behaviours.

As to 'authoring' a book on bullying, I believe there are only two kinds of people who have the credibility to write such a book: they're the men and women who have the academic qualifications to know how to emotionally support people who are being abused, and they're people who've been abused.

I'm from the latter category.

How to get the best out of this book:

This is a collection of personal experiences I've had over the years when dealing with people who would try to minimize and abuse me, not only on the home front but also in business and personal relationships.

I'll share the tips and survival tools I've picked up from the hundreds of workshops I've attended over the years as I learned how not to be the unwitting target of someone's abuse.

I eventually trained to be a counsellor, so it's also a collection of stories from people I've worked with to help them learn how to stand up for themselves.

On returning to the workplace after my 17-year marriage ended, I was staggered to see the toxicity that went on in the corporate world, so I'll share stories of people who were struggling with conflict and bullying in their workplaces.

The aim of the book is to give the reader tools, tips, ideas and strategies for dealing with any situation in their lives, be that at home or at work. If we're being made to feel uncomfortable, we need strategies for tackling the situation otherwise the situation will continue, it will get worse, and we will get sick.

I offer processes you can use if you fear you're managing a dysfunctional/abusive team and tips you can use if you believe you are the target of abuse from a work colleague or boss.

I'll share strategies I've used when speaking at conferences about conflict, bullying and toxic behaviours where people invariably stay behind to say, 'I need your help'.

You may be tempted to rush straight to the chapter on 'what to say, how to say it and when to say it', I urge you to read the lead-up chapters before that chapter because preparing for a difficult conversation is vital. It's really important not to rush in, totally ill prepared. The more information you have on who the person is, how they're likely to react and what to do if the conversation takes a nasty turn, the more successful the outcome will be and the more confidence you will gain, particularly if you realise that you have more than one person you need to talk to.

You'll find exercises scattered throughout the book. You can do these as you go or leave them till you've finished reading the entire book.

Once you've read the book keep it by you and open a page a day. The tips, tools and stories will be a comfort as you tackle this new skill of no longer being a doormat.

Take comfort from realizing that you're not a weak person, or a wimp or a patsy, you're a person doing the very best you can to become the best person you can.

I've used various real-life case studies, but the names of the people in those stories have all been changed.

Sticks and stones

The childhood nursery rhyme tells us:

> *Sticks and stones may break my bones,*
> *but names will never hurt me.*

The sad thing is, that names *do* hurt us. It may be a parent telling us we'll never amount to anything: a school friend telling us no one likes us: a work colleague telling us we are stupid or a significant other calling us names that belittle us.

I had a friend whose husband actually introduced her to people as 'his maggot' and I never once saw her stand up to him. I knew this couple well: I knew both of their family backgrounds.

Rick, the husband, had a very dominating mother and a passive father; he also had a brilliantly academic older sister. He spent his entire life being compared unfavourably to his sister, so I believe he took his unresolved female stuff from his childhood into his marriage. Vikki, his wife, had a belligerent father and a passive mother. She learned from her mother that it wasn't worth rocking the boat. So she didn't.

The problem for this couple is that they both have major health issues. They're now in their 70s and still do what they've always done to each other. Neither of them has ever changed their behaviours, though he did stop calling her his maggot, so I guess that's better than nothing.

Some people change when they see the light, some when they feel the heat, some people simply never change. In any family, bit by bit, a lifetime of put-downs has an effect. It wears us down, it wipes out our energy, it erases our sense of worth and our self-esteem plummets.

Throughout this book I'll explain:

- Why you can't excuse or rescue people who make you the target of their angst
- What to say when people put you down, minimise you, ignore you or bully you
- How to say what you need to say to people who treat you badly
- When to say what you need to say and how not to slip back into patterns of behaviour where you attract abusers over and over again, because if you don't learn how to stand up for yourself, you **will** attract abusers again and again and again.

If you're still with me, you're in the right book.

'The only people who get upset about you setting boundaries are the ones who were benefitting from you having none.'

Marloes De Vries

WARNING

THIS BOOK DOES NOT DEAL WITH
SCHOOL BULLYING, NOR DOES IT
DEAL WITH PHYSICAL ABUSE.

There are contact details in the resource area at the back of the book should you be dealing with either situation

HOW THE CHAPTERS UNFOLD

We're all products of our early beginnings, so in chapter one I concentrate on you the reader. I encourage you to investigate the first seven years of your life; the family you were born into; the era you were born, the culture you were born into and even your place in the family. All these aspects of your life form the beginnings of who you are.

All families have 'patterns' of how things get done, their beliefs, what they expect of their children if they are to fit in with their corner of society.

These early beginnings affect us as we grow into adulthood, as we start thinking about jobs or career paths, and they massively affect us as we start forming intimate relationships.

In Chapter 2, I explore self-esteem; what it is and how having a poor self-esteem seriously affects all aspects of our lives. I explore why we're all so different personality-wise: why some types of people seriously annoy us while others are so like us. I look at who we are attracted to and how we can learn to get on with the awkward people in our lives.

In Chapter 3, I move from uncomfortable behaviours in our homes to unacceptable behaviours in the workplace and the weird similarities we'll discover between the two.

I share exercises I conduct when working with teams experiencing conflict so they have the knowledge and skills to rise above personality clashes and find ways to create a more supportive and inclusive environment.

Teams need different personalities; if we all thought and behaved the same way, imagine not only how boring that would be but also how unproductive it would be. So, in this chapter, I show the reader how to value those differences rather than find them an irritant.

I then discuss the signs of a toxic workplace and the strange trait of projection; why some people accuse others in the team of the very behaviours they themselves are guilty of and how to deal with that.

I show the reader how to create a framework for their team so poor behaviours are eliminated and how they can create a set of ground rules to go forward as a healthy team minus all the gossip bitching and back-biting.

Chapter 4 deals with bullying at work. What bullying is and what it isn't. I explain the cost of bullying and the terrible effect it has on the target of the bully. I explain the difference between bullying and harassment and bullying and narcissism, and there are differences. I explain why sexual harassment in the workplace is totally unacceptable.

It's in this chapter that I investigate why some people become bullies and the effects not only of bullying on their targets, but also how their behaviours affect the bully in the long run. I researched whether bullies can change their behaviour and share the results of that research.

I share ways to ensure the naysayers, bullies and abusers give you a wide birth because you are now way too strong to get sucked into their games.

In Chapter 5, I share the strategies for dealing with obnoxious people. I share what to do, what to say, what not to say, and how to deal with the reactions you'll get from daring to stand up to someone. Because there will be reactions.

I share ways to set boundaries with people who would abuse you or use you. I show you how to own your part in the problem, because it really does take two to tango.

In Chapter 6, I talk about forgiveness. If you've been abused as a child, it's really hard to forgive your abuser, particularly if it was a parent who abused you. But forgiveness is vital. If we don't learn to forgive, the abuser doesn't know or care, but our bodies know. We store that hurt and pain for years, some people have stored their hurt for their entire lives; experience all manner of health problems and as a result, have never fulfilled their potential.

In Chapter 7, I remind you that you're never too old and it's never too late to do some of those things you dreamed of doing when you were younger before life and other people's dramas got in the way.

I show you how to rebuild your self-esteem and to make sure your self-esteem stays intact forever because once you refuse to be a victim, or a target or someone's dumping ground, your life will change beyond all recognition.

Chapter 8 challenges you to feel the fear and do it anyway. To take those first steps into your purpose and your destiny. It encourages you to do regular mental, physical and even spiritual checks: to believe in miracles and to know that you are divinely guided and supported.

Chapter 9 offers you further resources. I share great quotes if you ever feel yourself slipping back. I share my own 40-year reading list and I offer further reading suggestions for specific areas I've covered in the book if you want to delve more deeply into a particular topic.

You'll find further resources on any number of topics. I've listed some resources if your children are being bullied. I share an array of templates you can access for some of the work areas of your life. I list the various counselling services available if you need to physically talk to someone.

I end the book with the strange things that happened to cause me to write this book; a book I didn't even have on my horizon.

I then offer my heartfelt thanks to the amazing people I've met along my own journey of learning how to deal with bullies, narcissists and downright nasty people.

And finally, there's a whole section on the references I used to investigate the topic of bullies, narcissists and harassers.

They are amongst us, sadly.

> 'Some people are in such utter darkness that they will burn you just to see a light. Try not to take it personally.'
>
> KAMAND KOJOURI

CHAPTER 1
FIRST BASE: UNDERSTANDING YOURSELF

'Forgive those who didn't know how to love you, they were teaching you how to love yourself.'

—Ryan Elliot

UNDERSTANDING THE FIRST 0-7 YEARS OF OUR LIVES

Our first seven years don't begin when we're born, they begin when we are conceived. Even from the instant of conception, a foetus is taking in messages from their mother.

If our mother already has too many children and is exhausted, we're absorbing that exhaustion and sadness in the womb. If our mother was in a difficult marriage; was planning to leave and then finds herself pregnant and stuck, once again, her resentment will be channelled into us.

If our mother is young, had a drunken one-night stand and now finds herself pregnant, we will absorb that fear and possibly even self-disgust and bitter regret.

So even before we're born, we may have picked up that:

- My mother doesn't want me
- My mother just tried to abort me
- I'm a nuisance

Alternatively, we may be our parents' last ditch stand to have a son when they already have five daughters, and here I am, another daughter. Or I'm another son when they desperately wanted a daughter. There may be a sense of disappointment the second our parents know our gender, which the unborn child will absorb.

We may have been born into a family where females in the family are second-class citizens, are kept in their place, and have zero say in anything of importance, so even before we are born, we're at a disadvantage. Not a great start.

OR, our beginnings may be the exact opposite.

Our parents may have been trying to conceive for many years and we pop into their lives and the love and joy they feel for us is staggering. They're ultra-protective of us, we get all the right foods and nourishment. We are so loved and wanted and we haven't even been born yet.

The downside of being desperately wanted is that we may feel smothered.

In the first scenario, once we're born, our relationship with our mother may be difficult, she may do her best for us, but we may not feel any real love or joy in our coming into the world. As a result of that lack of love, we may spend a huge part of the rest of our lives searching for that elusive unconditional love.

Aristotle said, 'Give me a child till he's seven and I'll show you the man'.

From conception to seven, our messages about who we are and our 'worth' come from the love and acceptance we do or don't receive from our parents.

Until seven years old, we don't have the ability to rationalize any of the things we hear being said to us or from the way we are treated. We are giant sponges absorbing everything that comes our way without the reasoning skills to separate the good from the bad.

Around the age of seven we develop the beginnings of our rationalization skills. We're now able to view a situation and to put a tiny amount of enquiry into what we're witnessing.

We'll be at school by now and will be noticing other children acting differently. The confident ones, those whose parents encouraged them, will already be doing better at school than the kids who pretty much had to fend for themselves.

We may start being invited to other people's homes for a sleep-over, so we'll experience strange ways of doing things and different ways of family members treating each other. Dinner in our home may be at a certain time and at the table, whereas this family I'm staying with seem to live on takeaways, eat any old time and eat in front of the television.

OUR FAMILY OF ORIGIN

In our early years, everything we believe to be true comes from our family of origin. We inherently trust everything our parents, grandparents, even uncles and aunts tell us. We do what they do, we do what they tell us to do. We're being immersed in this grounding which will affect us for the rest of our lives.

LEARNED BEHAVIOURS

We all have behaviours and practices that we picked up from that family of origin. From simple things like how to fold towels, to who does the cooking or who cleans the toilet, and most importantly, how to resolve conflict. Or not.

We naturally fear going against our family: we fear that if we do that, we risk being ridiculed or even cut off if we rebel against their expectations of us.

For girls, it could be:

- Be seen and not heard
- Know your place
- Girls do the housework and boys help in the garden
- Don't be too pushy, you'll put men off
- Don't aim too high, you don't want to be disappointed OR
- Aim high, there's nothing a girl can't achieve

For boys it may be the opposite:

- Boys do the outside work
- They learn to fix things
- Boys have to be tough
- Boys are never expected to cook or clean, that's women's work
- Men will become the breadwinners, so they need to select a safe and secure profession

If a child sees a parent throwing tantrums or having major meltdowns, which result in them getting their own way, then children will learn that bullying and temper tantrums work; they will then take those tantrums into the schoolyard; into their relationships and into their work life, because they've learned that they work.

There are acknowledged differences in the way males and females bully others. Boys tend to experience more physical bullying while girls suffer more name calling and shaming.

Whatever our family taught us or allowed us to get away with, those recordings are embedded into our brains.

LIMITING BELIEFS

These learned behaviours then start a recording in our heads, which plays on a regular basis:

- I mustn't be loud or rock the boat
- I must be ladylike
- I'm not as important as my brother

Finally, we head into the workplace, where if we thought high school and Uni were confusing and confronting, entering the workplace can feel as if we've landed in an alternate universe. At least in our strange family, we knew our place. We knew what would happen if we spoke out of turn or didn't do our chores.

At work no one seems to tell us anything, we're expected to work things out for ourselves and then when we do we get called out by our grumpy old boss for not doing a good job when we were never told how to do the job in the first place.

My 'black belt' granddaughter is waiting to head to Uni and has taken a part-time job in a retail shop where she is being told by rude customers how dumb she is and how stupid. My suggestion to her was to mentally channel her 'black belt' every time someone is rude to her. She doesn't have to be rude back, but she can rise above the abuse.

If your childhood was painful, sad and lonely, I'm sad for you. If you went through a childhood being neglected, left hungry, cold or berated. I'm sad for you. But you're still here, still functioning

Whatever your 0–7 years were; whatever strange family you find yourself in; whether you're living out the message that you're stupid and useless, or whether you've been told you're amazing and can be anything you choose to be, this is your life. Unless you decide differently.

If it's working, you probably won't be reading this book. If you're reading this book, then congratulate yourself on getting this far in life.

Most of all, though, please remember that your parents had their own 0–7 years, just as their parents had theirs.

> *'We repeat what we don't repair'*
> —Sharon Martin

PLACE IN THE FAMILY

Our place in the family has significant relevance.

If you're the oldest child in your family, you'll be expected to be more responsible than your siblings. Middle children confess to feeling invisible, youngest child tends to have more freedom. Only children tend to feel lonely and given they are surrounded by older family members, tend to be more serious than kids with brothers and sisters.

Time passes and our lives settle into the pattern of our family, our culture and our religion.

If our parents taught us to expect certain things about society, and what we're experiencing bears no resemblance to what they taught us, our parents may fall off their pedestal as we start to feel like a fish out of water.

We may start to resent our parents, rationalizing that they lied to us or that they didn't prepare us for any of the challenges we're trying to deal with.

THE ERA YOU WERE BORN

My grandmother was born at the turn of the 21st century. She survived two world wars and the Great Depression. She was not expected to work but rather to get married, have children and keep the home fires burning.

My mother was born in the mid-1920s. She was encouraged to get a job but was expected to leave that job once she married.

I was born just after the Second World War, a time of food rationing, shortages of everything, a time when nothing was ever thrown out or wasted. I still can't bear to throw food out. Leftovers can always be turned into something, a pie, a casserole, a curry.

Women of my generation were given three career choices: secretary, nurse, teacher, and were expected to leave the workforce once they became pregnant.

My children were born in the 70s. My daughter was born into the generation of girls that were told they could be anything and do anything and so when she became a mother, she was *expected* to be everything to everybody. To be a mother, to be a full-time worker, to be the one who picks up most of the household chores and to work right up until a couple of days before giving birth.

A massively tall order.

FATHERS AND SONS

It isn't just women who have had societal expectations thrust onto them. My partner of 30 years was born in the last year of the Second World War; his father had been a soldier who came home very rarely and very briefly. Warren's father lost his father when he was just 12 years old.

On his father's return from fighting, he now had a one-year-old son he barely knew. So many men came back from the war with what we now know as PTSD; they were damaged men, and if not damaged, then they were certainly affected by what they'd seen and had to do.

Warren ended up being an only child whose mother doted on him while his dad spent the entire 65 years of his marriage trying to be number one in his wife's book. He never achieved that status, he always felt he was an outsider and he took that out on Warren.

Warren's father was a coach builder, a highly qualified mechanic, a handyman extraordinaire and an amazing artist. Warren became a very successful accountant and franchisor but a man not to be let loose anywhere near a hammer. If he hammered a nail into a piece of wood, the ambulance service was put on alert in case he severed an artery. Another failure on Warren's part in his father's eyes.

Warren's father lost his dad when he was 12 years old, Warren never found his. They simply never built a relationship.

So it really isn't just women who can be minimized and ignored, husbands and sons can suffer the same fate because of circumstances beyond their control.

THE CULTURE YOU WERE BORN INTO

It seems that there are two distinct groups of women who attend my courses.

Young women born into cultures where women are considered second-class citizens: the 'be seen and not heard' of my grandmother's generation and older European women who came from generations where nothing was expected of them, whose kids have now left home and are looking at the rest of their lives with trepidation.

They may be widows, divorcees or older women looking after elderly partners. For them, they feel their lives are empty, they have nothing to joyously get up in the morning for other than more of the same.

What is certain is that all of the women who attend my sessions are not happy with their lives, yet all of them express massive amounts of guilt because they're supposed to be happy with their lot. So many of them admit to being on anti-depressants.

WHEN CULTURES COLLIDE

My daughter became engaged to a very handsome Middle Eastern man. He was charming and personable and clearly adored my daughter. In one of the conversations I had with him, I became incredibly alarmed. He told me that he had an uncle who loved his wife so much he didn't let her out of the house in case she might be subjected to humiliation.

My response to him as he proudly recounted that horror story was that his aunt wasn't 'loved', she was incarcerated.

I now seriously feared for my daughter and urged her to watch the movie 'Not without my daughter'. I have no idea whether she did, but I learned later that the women in his family suggested she make the most of her freedom before she became his wife because she would not be allowed the freedom she was used to.

One of the women in the family, shared her story with my daughter of how she asked her husband if she could join a women's gym and was told categorically that she was not allowed.

Whatever caused my daughter to break off the engagement, I was so relieved when she did.

I have to take great care teaching women how to stand up for themselves because the last thing I would want to do is to endanger them. However, my rationale is that they're on my course so are clearly ready to make some changes in their lives, it's my role to facilitate whatever changes they want to make in a way that will not endanger them or their children.

Meet Susan

Susan was a friend of mine during our college years. She was an only child born to older parents and was worshipped. Tragically her father had died when she was seven years old and because her father had been a mason, she qualified for a free scholarship at a boarding school too far away for her to be able to travel home for weekends.

She and her mother never built a strong relationship; her mother was possessive and fussy and very nervy, so as Susan got older, she preferred not to go home for holidays other than for the long Christmas break. When she was home she wasn't allowed out on her own, wherever she went her mother had to go with her.

After finishing her education, Susan literally went wild. She had been 'contained' within the boarding school system and by her mother since she was seven, and now she had absolute freedom. She partied hard, drank hard, often didn't come home for days and when she did venture home, was in such a sorry state her mother would be furious with her and another round of fighting and misery would ensue.

Susan escaped into what looked like a great marriage. She married a handsome naval officer who spent long spells at sea.

When he was home Susan was 'contained' again, she wasn't allowed to see her friends; was kept on a minimum amount of money and had to account for every penny she spent, and she was not allowed to go out unless he was with her.

Susan committed suicide at just 27. What a tragic waste of a beautiful life.

> 'You can have a pet zebra and put that zebra into a small cage every day and tell the zebra that you love it, but no matter how you and the zebra love each other, the fact remains that the zebra should be let out of that cage and should belong to someone who can treat it better, the way it should be treated, someone who can make it happy.'
>
> — C. JoyBell C.

MY OWN 0-7 YEARS

I'm illegitimate and was born in a small town at a time in society when it was not cool to be illegitimate. I thought my mother was my sister and that her younger sister and older brother were my brother and sister. I called my grandparents mum and dad, and I lived with them believing they were my parents until I was six. This way of dealing with illegitimacy was common in families for hundreds of years.

I don't remember my mother very much in my early years, she seemed to waft into our home now and again smelling and looking gorgeous, and then would waft out again.

Suddenly, I was being bought a new school uniform and was told that I was now going to live with Mavis (my new-found mother) and her new husband.

I was absolutely blessed in those first six years of living with my amazing grandparents. In them, I'd had the best mum and dad anyone could wish for, however, my life was about to take a dark turn.

My newfound mother pretty much ignored me, she was a social butterfly, rarely home, but worse, I now had a stepfather who emotionally, psychologically and sexually abused me for years.

I escaped at 18, never really understanding why they took me away from my grandparents. I was told by an aunt many years later that having a child that couldn't live with them qualified them for a brand-new state house. Which explained everything.

I'd been of use to them.

I never knew who my real father was. I asked Mavis several times but was met with such an angry reaction I stopped asking. My mother had been in the services during the Second World War and I was clearly conceived at the end of that war, so chances are my real father would have been a serviceman.

I firmly believe that if I hadn't had those first six amazing years with my grandparents, I wouldn't have survived living with these two awful people. I escaped by joining the Women's Royal Navy and strangely followed in my mother's footsteps.

I eventually met and married a man who came from a similarly dysfunctional background and because of that, we were determined not to make the same mistakes. For the first 10 years of our marriage, we were really, truly happy.

What we didn't realize was that we had each brought our own baggage into the relationship without the skills to be able to work through our differences. We both came from families where yelling and abusing were the norm and so we carried on the tradition.

I read that relationships are like the maths equation: $½ \times ½ = ¼$. So I brought my half of hurt and neglect and joined forces with his half of hurt and neglect and instead of us making up a whole, we were left with one quarter, which ultimately wasn't enough solidity to sustain our relationship.

Ten years into our marriage we had an opportunity to move from the UK to New Zealand with our then 3-year-old and 1-year-old.

I watched as my husband changed personality. I've never been sure why he changed, whether it was because we were now away from family support, though I suspect it was because he saw wealth in New Zealand that he could only dream of, and it changed his personality.

I was now back to experiencing the exact same neglect I'd had from my mother. My husband was never home, he started mixing with people I found shallow, but they were rich and he was besotted with them. I quickly dropped in rankings from wife to poorly paid handmaiden.

After a particularly miserable spell in our marriage, he asked for some 'time-out'. His rationale was that he was going through some strange psychological stuff and felt he needed time to sort himself out.

I was totally sympathetic. I got it and I desperately wanted my old husband back. He had a couple of weeks away and came back sorry for the way he'd been treating not just me but also the kids. We had a year of being almost back to normal and then he asked for another 'time-out'.

This time I said that if he left, he would no longer be welcome back because this wasn't fair on me, and it was horribly unsettling for the kids. He left and I took the keys to our home back off him. I'd discovered that his 'time-out' was to spend time with another woman.

At the time refusing to take my husband back was an incredibly brave decision, however, I was determined I would not put up with being used this way and I couldn't stand by as my kids were seeing him coming and going and not understanding why.

Then reality hit home, I had obsolete skills, no bank account, two teenagers, a clapped-out old car and a dog that ate everyone's socks.

I stepped out into a future that was terrifying. I'd been kept down for so many years I had no idea that I actually had a brain, even though I'd had rapid promotion when I was in the WRNS. That was now a distant memory.

My self-esteem had been at rock bottom for so long that I wasn't sure I was going to be able to climb out of the pit, but deep inside a little voice had been growing. I'd had those amazing first six years, and my grounding had been rock-solid. I knew I deserved better.

For each and every one of us, there comes a time when we reach our 'enough' stage and I knew that wherever I was going had to be better than the shallow life I was living. By making that decision, it was as if a cage door had been opened for me.

I flew.

My new journey started by going back into secretarial work; I became PA to a human resources manager; became a personnel manager in my own right, moved up the corporate ladder to become HR manager in a computer company to finally, in less than ten years, I set up my own HR consultancy specializing in working with high performing teams.

Over my life, I've had to learn to understand those 0–7 years. I had to understand why my marriage failed. I wanted to make sense of why I stayed in an unhappy marriage for so long to make sure I didn't make the same mistake again.

I'm clearly a slow learner because I repeated my mistakes several times over the next few years as I started dating again. A friend had once said that she 'got into relationships too fast and got out too slow'.

I got faster at getting out of any relationship that belittled me.

If you've repeated your mistakes several times, don't fret, it's normal. Sometimes we really do need a whack on the side of the head till we get it that we are 'worth' respect, and if we don't respect ourselves, no one else will respect us.

Finally, I got it.

> *When they say 'It runs in the family' tell them,*
> *'And this is where it runs out'*
> —Abhi Raynot

MY FIRST WOMEN'S GROUPS

I'd been working as an HR manager in the corporate world and became the first and only woman on an all-male senior management team in the very young computer sector. I was excited at the prospect of a new challenge after having spent many years working in manufacturing plants. The fact that I was doubling my salary and getting a very flash company car was a seductive lure.

Within a week of taking on the job I realized I'd just made a massive mistake.

As women, I think we 'feel' energy. If we're ever house hunting, we tend to pick on the vibes of the houses we view. Even on the very first day, the vibes in this company were not pleasant. As I was being taken around and introduced to various managers, let's say I wasn't feeling particularly welcome. Sadly, I hadn't picked up on that energy at the interview stage.

I knew I had to get two years on my CV to maintain any level of credibility but had no idea how I would survive two years.

Fortunately, one of the less pretentious and prickly senior managers heard about the work I'd done with self-managing teams in my previous manufacturing position and asked if I would work with his team. He was based in Wellington, so I spent the next year commuting to Wellington and escaping the atmosphere of the Auckland head office.

Once the work with his team was completed, I started to plan my escape. I decided to negotiate my own redundancy. It was clear that taking on an HR manager (female) had been a PR exercise insisted on by the American head office, so when I asked for a year's salary for six months of work to complete a project that had to be done by law, my offer was accepted.

I flew out of another cage.

By now I'd decided I wanted to work for myself, so I set up my own HR consultancy and began the painfully slow and expensive journey of marketing and selling myself. While I set up my new business, I still had to eat and feed my kids and pay the mortgage, so until I was successful in winning some HR contracts, I had to find a way to keep money coming in. I leaned on my counselling training and set up my first ever workshops for women.

My first few sessions were totally experimental. I didn't even know enough to send out a pre-course questionnaire, so on the very first session I asked each attendee to tell the group what was going on in their lives and what they wanted from my course.

Every single woman wanted help to deal with some aspect of conflict occurring in their lives. Mostly from their significant others, but often from close family or friends but for some, with difficult work colleagues.

I built my courses around teaching people what to say in difficult circumstances, how to say what they needed to say and what to do if the conversations turned nasty.

Learning to have such conversations works whether you're a parent with a troublesome relative; a person in a debilitating marriage; a boss having challenges with difficult workers or an employee having challenges with a co-worker or autocratic boss is vital. If we don't learn to stand up for ourselves, whether that's in a home or work situation, we literally become doormats.

> *'Many neglected and abused children grow up to be adults who are afraid to take risks of striking out on their own. Many will*

remain dependent on their abusive parents and unable to separate from them. Others leave their abusive parents only to attach themselves to a partner who is controlling.'

— Beverly Engel, *The Nice Girl Syndrome: Stop Being Manipulated and Abused—And Start Standing Up for Yourself*

ENDING THE PATTERNS THAT HAVE TAKEN OVER OUR LIVES FOR BETTER OR WORSE

Every family has their own distinct 'patterns', from the way we wash dishes, to who cleans the toilets, even down to how we vote.

I remember a friend telling me that she was going to vote for a Labour candidate in the general election because her father would turn in his grave if she voted any other way. How's that for a pattern?

Some patterns are harmless. Who cares whether you fold your towels a certain way or go to a certain church because your family has always attended that church. It's absolutely OK to follow patterns that suit you; that give you peace and a sense of security. It's when that pattern gives you none of those things. It's when you feel stifled, or pressured, or uncomfortable or even brain-washed that it isn't OK.

Once we're adults, it's up to us how we choose to live our lives. No parent, partner, sibling, community or culture should be in charge of the decisions we make about our life and how we live it.

'Identifying the pattern is awareness; choosing not to repeat the cycle is growth.'
—Billy Chapata

CHAPTER 2
WHY CAN'T PEOPLE BE MORE LIKE ME?

'All the people like us are WE and everyone else is THEY'

—Rudyard Kipling

I'M OK, YOU'RE NOT SO HOT

The information in this next chapter taught me so much about myself, my personality, my ex-husband's personality, my horrible stepfather's personality and even my mother's personality.

Within four years of ending my marriage, I'd become a personnel manager in a manufacturing plant. After my military service, I'd actually trained as a work study engineer with the Johnson & Johnson company, so moving into personnel was a very natural transition. My role was to help a manufacturing plant deal with high absenteeism, high turnover and a high accident rate.

I had no idea how invaluable my work study background, combined with my counselling and relationship training was going to be as I worked with teams.

When someone in the workplace complains to me about a colleague who is giving them grief, I ask them, 'Who, in your family, does this person remind you of?' I'm still staggered when I see the realization slowly dawn on them that the person is like their mother, or sister, or an uncle who used to taunt them.

I'm constantly amazed that assertiveness isn't taught in schools; I'm even more amazed that once kids reach adulthood (18 years of age) they aren't profiled, so they understand themselves but also understand how other people function.

It's fairly predictable that if we've never understood or taught how to deal with that angry father or passive mother, or bossy sister, we'll meet that same personality at the alter or in the workplace.

As my work began with the various departments and teams in this manufacturing plant, one department had turnover so high the general manager asked me to investigate to find out why.

I'd recently attended a workshop on 'profiling', a tool that was adorably called 'the DOPE test'.

There are now hundreds of profiling tools available, all based on four personality types, in this case, Doves, Owls, Peacocks and Eagles. We have all four of the personalities in us, but we will have a dominant trait and a weakness, our least trait.

Doves are gentle people, the carers, the kind people in your life and work team, the people who will calm the troubled waters if arguments break out between team (or family) members. Doves are naturally attracted to nursing, child-care or counselling roles.

Owls are detail people, the dot the I's and cross the T's people. Owls are notoriously risk averse, cautious people and invariably take on careers in accounting, insurance, banking and even health and safety.

Peacocks are always loud, always fun. They're party people. They are the members of a team who bring jokes, boundless energy and outrageous ideas. Peacocks are naturally drawn into sales roles.

Eagles are get-things-done people, the people who thrive on deadlines and quantifiable results. They're quite naturally bossy people, those co-workers in your team who can't seem to help taking over running everything. They're also accomplished delegators.

In the following diagram, you will see a comparison of the DOPE test and a profiling tool called DISC, which is probably the most prodigiously used profiling tool in the workplace but not nearly as much fun to teach or learn as the DOPE test.

Doves are classed as 'steady' people in DISC language. Owls are classified as 'compliance' people, Peacocks are categorized as 'influencers' and Eagles are categorized as 'dominant' personalities.

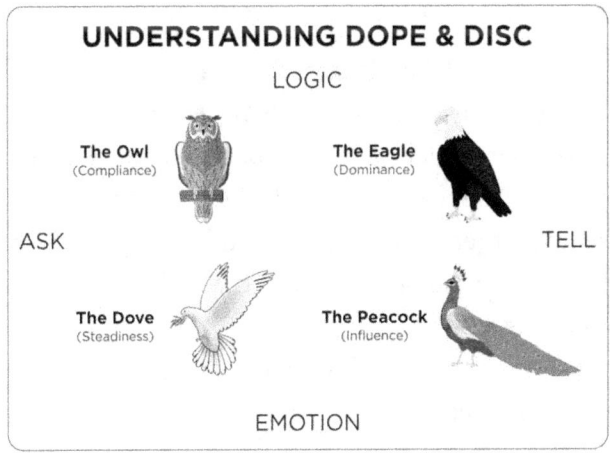

You'll notice in the diagram the similarities between Owls and Eagles who both tend to make their decisions based on logic; while

Doves and Peacocks make decisions based on emotion. They talk about having a 'gut feel'.

We then see similarities between Doves and Owls in that they're low assertive, they tend to ask permission to do things, whereas Peacocks and Eagles are high assertive and tend to tell people what to do and when to do it—usually the poor, unfortunate Owls and Doves.

I went on to spend 30 years specializing in working with high performing teams and always teach teams the value of profiling.

Everything I did to encourage a team to work more cohesively, to better understand each other and to recruit more effectively was based on them understanding the different personalities. To know and understand themselves, for better or worse, but also to understand the other personalities in their team and who they are most likely to clash with.

I would also show teams why we need each personality 'type' because if a team has:

- No Owl there will be a lack of detail and research. Teams lacking a detail person invariably have very poor systems.
- No Dove, there will be a lack of 'people' care, whether that's within the team itself or of their customers
- No Peacock, there will be no fun, and energy levels may be low because it really is the Peacock who brings the spark that lights us all
- No Eagle, we will inevitably have vague deadlines and poor timekeeping

However, when pressure is brought to bear on each of us, we each have a distinct way of expressing our stress:

Owls will go into hiding: they'll close the door to their office if they have an office or will put up mental shutters if they work in an open office; Doves become emotional and teary; Peacocks tend to act out, become even louder than normal and can become drama queens; while Eagles become even more bossy and intimidating than normal. Yelling for them is simply how they express frustration. Being yelled at is terrifying for Owls and Doves.

What I learned about myself when I attended the course with three other personnel managers was that I'm primarily Dove. I am a caring person, I can get teary if I'm feeling overpowered or stressed and I do get upset if people yell at me. I know at first glance I can be seen as a push-over.

NB: *Doves are the most likely targets in a workplace to be bullied. Which is sad and tragic. They are gentle people, caring people, yet are viewed as a soft target for people who are bullies and who always seem to need to vent their spleen on someone.*

Being a Dove I've had my fair share of being yelled at, however, what I also learned through profiling, is that my second personality trait is Eagle. People can only push me so far before I react. Hence me telling my ex-husband that if he left this time he would not be allowed back, and he wasn't.

Have a look again at the various personality styles and rank them in the order you think you have them. Check with people who know you well, ask them if this is who they think you are. They will tell you.

My traits, in order are Dove, Eagle, Peacock, Owl. I'm hopeless with detail. Numbers give me a migraine, yet I'm brilliant with deadlines.

If you've now worked out your personality style, consider next, in your work setting, who gives you the most grief?

We have the greatest conflict with our diametric opposite personality:

Doves are intimidated by Eagles, and Eagles think Doves are wimps. Owls resent Peacocks and Peacocks think Owls are nitpickers.

When working with teams, I teach Owls and Doves to speak up more frequently, while I ask Eagles and Peacocks to learn to listen. Something they are not good at doing. I go so far when working with teams to insist on them using a 'talking stick' so everyone in the team or meeting is given the opportunity to be heard.

Once I understood my own personality, I decided to work out the traits of my family:

My grandfather was an Owl.

My grandmother was a Dove.

My mother was a Peacock.

My ex-husband is a Peacock.

My stepfather was an Eagle.

My mother had kept me really short of money and was never home so first time around, I married a man who kept me really short of money and was never home.

My biggest learning from working and understanding profiling was that I'd married someone who totally resembled my mother!

'Be yourself; everyone else is taken.'
—Oscar Wilde

UNDERSTANDING THE DIFFERENCE BETWEEN ASSERTIVENESS AND AGGRESSION

Definitions:

- Assertiveness is the quality of being confident and unafraid to say what you want to say or to believe what you believe
- Aggression is the spoken or physical behaviour that is threatening or involves harming someone or something

I've worked with many people who presented as timid little mice, who, once they'd had a few sessions with me became roaring lions. We don't want people to be timid little mice but going from one extreme to the polar opposite in a matter of weeks isn't the intention either. We have to find the balance.

Helping people to find their voices takes time. It's new to them. They've probably never said 'No' in their entire lives and a little bit like learning to drive a car, you start off learning how to use the lower gears first before you try out reverse and three-point turns.

This is why I always recommend trying out their chosen phrases with a trusted friend. To rehearse what they want to say. To get clear what they actually want from the other person.

So many women simply say 'I want to be loved'. OK, how do you want to be shown that?

Men invariably say 'I want to be respected', OK how are you currently not being respected?

> *'If you don't ask for what you want you won't get it, it's as simple as that. People are lousy mind-readers.'*
> —Unknown

UNDERSTANDING THE CRITICAL IMPORTANCE OF HAVING A HEALTHY SELF-ESTEEM

Being belittled, minimized, ignored and abused will affect our self-worth, our self-esteem and ultimately our mental and physical health.

I've had many conversations about the difference between self-esteem and self-worth, and according to author Hailey Shafir of 'Choosing Therapy', self-esteem and self-worth are related but have important differences.

> 'Self-esteem describes how you think and feel about yourself, which changes based on mood, circumstance, performance, or the approval of others. Self-worth is a more global and stable form of self-esteem that comes from knowing and believing in your worth as a person.'

And so we live out our lives based on all manner of messages we've received from our family, from our friends, from our workmates. Some of which are true, some of which are their interpretation of who we are.

> 'Family is supposed to be our safe haven. Very often it's the place where we find the deepest heartache'
> —Ilanya Vanzant

A SELF-ESTEEM TEST

Answer the following questions and rank them on a scale of 0–10: 0–5 if you absolutely agree, 6–10 if you absolutely disagree.

1. I've achieved absolutely nothing in my life so far. I'm a loser.
2. I cry for days if someone criticizes me.
3. I come from a family of failures.
4. I can't stop thinking about all the bad things happening in my life.
5. I have no idea how to say NO.
6. I constantly compare myself to others and come up wanting.
7. I have real difficulty making decisions.
8. I really dislike myself.
9. If someone pays me a compliment, I will negate it.
10. I know I'll never succeed at anything.

If you've consistently scored yourself from 0–5 then you know you have really low self-esteem. But there's always hope and there's always tomorrow. You can rebuild yourself.

> 'You can't love someone else until you love yourself'
> —Psychology Today

CHAPTER 3
HOW TO ADDRESS INAPPROPRIATE BEHAVIOURS IN YOUR TEAM

'If someone treats you badly, just remember that there's something wrong with them, not you. Normal people don't go around destroying other human beings.'

—Rob Dial

SIGNS OF A TOXIC WORK ENVIRONMENT

My traditional calls for help are invariably from an owner, franchisor, team leader or manager. Someone who has either inherited a troublemaker or two; someone who has recruited a person who isn't working out, or someone who has promoted a person into a position of management who morphs into a power-mad monster.

I've worked with teams of all shapes and sizes, all colours and creeds. All my work starts with that 'Help' call. I've worked in the banking sector, the insurance industry; the concrete sector; real estate, manufacturing, technology and even with a rugby team.

My strangest call though, was from a spiritual counsellor, who was the president of an international spiritual group. I was speechless when she acknowledged that she was dealing with a couple of incredibly toxic people.

She acknowledged the group had their fair share of big noters; people who took credit for things someone else had done and people who were stabbing someone else in the back. A spiritual group! You would think they, of all people, would be above earthly tantrums. Not so.

However, sometimes, the person who is causing the mayhem is the owner, franchisor, team leader or manager. It can take a while for people to realise that they may be the problem.

There are some clear signs of a dysfunctional/toxic team:

1. Work overload leading to stress and absenteeism
2. Conflict between team members
3. No opportunity to raise concerns
4. Lack of recognition or ideas being stolen
5. Poor recruitment processes
6. Poor promotion decisions
7. A failure to deal with poor performance or unacceptable behaviours
8. Poor leadership
9. Poor communication
10. Lack of effective meetings
11. High turnover

If good personnel records are kept and monitored, the signs of a toxic team will be apparent in just a few months. Particularly if this is a large organization where comparisons can be made between a number of teams and departments.

These key indicators of a toxic environment need to be dealt with quickly.

If staff are overworked, then this serves no one. It will lead to burnout, high absenteeism and eventually people will leave. If there is conflict between team members, this needs to be dealt with; once again, conflict leads to stress, stress leads to absenteeism.

Every business needs to have a way for people to raise concerns; either via an effective HR person or anyone in senior management who will listen and take action.

Effective teams begin with good recruitment processes and a willingness to keep an eye on new recruits. Are new people brought into the team to become high performers, or are they just left to find their own way?

Promoting unsuitable people into management positions is a recipe for disaster. Power corrupts and total power corrupts totally. Promotions shouldn't just be about promoting high performers, people promoted into management need to have highly developed people skills.

If we've promoted people into a management position who are afraid to deal with their poor performers, poor performance will spread. If one person gets away with arriving late and leaving early every day, pretty soon you will have a whole department doing the same.

Leadership is about having a vision for the team—something more than just getting more stuff out the door. Is the manager a person who keeps up with trends and is aware of changing markets? Are they adaptable, responsive, and good listeners? Do they deal with issues or sweep them under the carpet? Do they play favourites and recruit 'yes' people? Are they just about bottom-line results, or do they care about their people?

Great managers are also great communicators; they don't leave people in the dark, and they don't hoard information thinking information is power.

Effective meetings are the lifeblood of good communication. Meetings should never be just about one person talking and everyone trying to stay awake. Great meetings are energizing and involve everyone feeling free to raise issues. Good and bad.

DEALING WITH CONFLICT IN TEAMS

I read the book *Why Teams Don't Work* when I was head down building teams and was concerned that I was wasting my life.

However, I realized it was a shock title to ensure people working in teams or with teams realized the complexities. And a quote from the book really made me chuckle:

> 'A team isn't any kind of device. It's much more than that—it's a surprising, perplexing, up-and-down, tragicomic, value-creating human thing. A human thing that needs a ton of attention, that has to be pampered, fed, stroked and even have its pen hosed out from time to time.'
>
> —*Why Teams Don't Work*, Harvey Robbins & Michael Finley

And for sure, I've 'hosed' out many teams over the years.

However, in the beginning, when I set up my own HR consultancy, I'd been marketing and promoting the concept of 'self-managed' teams, yet the amazing thing was that when I got my very first call from a potential business client, he asked if I could help with the conflict that was happening in his team.

And so my work helping teams experiencing conflict began.

I describe it as my day job (HR) and my night job (counselling) colliding.

I'd originally trained as a counsellor and had completed my training as a marriage guidance counsellor. I'd worked in couple counselling and even some family counselling, so in the early days of becoming a solo mum I'd run a few workshops for women until I got my first job in the business world.

Just as in a dysfunctional family, there will be signs of an unhappy team. In the workplace, the signs will be:

- High absenteeism
- High turnover
- High sickness rate
- Poor quality
- Poor productivity
- Low morale
- Zero creativity
- High litigation costs

When I'm invited to work with a team, I use very similar strategies to those I use when I'm working with a woman's group. I ask team members to define the behaviours they want in the team they work with and the behaviours they do not want.

The comments below came from a real-life team exercise. When asked, the team said these were the behaviours they did not want in their team:

EXERCISE: THE BEHAVIOURS WE DO NOT WANT IN THIS TEAM

* Going behind each other's backs. Rudeness, making others feel uncomfortable, impatience, negative attitudes. Excluding people, forming cliques, wasting time in meetings. Talking over each other, being dramatic. Harsh words, aggressive behaviours, control freaks, imposing ideas on others. Judging people, bullying, lying disrespecting. Gossiping. Not listening. Pity. Unprofessionalism. Arguments. Micro-managing. Talking about a team member in front of other team members. Not doing what you said you would do. Making assumptions. Not attending meetings. Coming unprepared to meetings. Not replying to emails. Having to chase people. People who don't want to learn.

EXERCISE: THE BEHAVIOURS WE DO WANT IN THIS TEAM

* Patience, kindness, understanding. Everyone being given the same opportunities. Being professional, team members taking their work seriously and being accountable. Commitment, flexibility, positivity, effective communication. Supportiveness. Actively listen to what people are saying. Keep an open mind. Be calm and respectful. Positive vibes. Respect. Fairness, working together with an end goal. Honesty, loyalty, punctuality. To have each other's backs. An opportunity to make suggestions and ask questions. Compassion. Shared responsibilities. Accept we are all different. Embrace each other's strengths.

EXERCISE: HOW TO CREATE A SET OF GROUND RULES

Having discussed all the aspects of behaviours they do and don't want in their team, I ask the team to then create a set of ground rules—rules they agree to abide by going forward.

This part of the exercise requires every member of the team to state 'the one thing above all else that's important to them':

- What's said here stays here (no gossip outside the room)
- We support each other no matter what
- If a person can't do the task they undertook to do, to let someone know
- To come to meetings having done their allocated tasks
- To come to meetings on time
- If one person is struggling, let us know so we can help
- If two people are in conflict offer to mediate
- If someone isn't performing offer to help

I then ask the team to put these ground rules up on the wall in their lunchroom and to have a copy on the table when they have their next meeting.

It isn't unusual to have a couple of team members opt out of the 'what I don't want in this team' exercise.

In my experience it isn't that they are cowards or shy, it's usually that they've never been asked to express an opinion and so invariably don't have an opinion. Possibly a left-over from their family where they were told 'girls are seen and not heard', or if it's a male who can't offer a ground rule, they may have had an overbearing father who came from the 'when I want your opinion, I'll ask for it' school of fatherhood.

I urge them to keep thinking about their ground rule and to feel free at any stage to bring it to the table to add to the existing ground rules.

ENSURING PEOPLE ABIDE BY THE GROUND RULES

I introduce a team to the phrase 'remember we said…' or 'remember we agreed…' because we don't change habits of a lifetime overnight. Sometimes, we slip back and need that reminder that, yes, we did agree we wouldn't do XYZ.

I also suggest the use of 'fines'.

If someone is late to the meeting, instigate a $5 fine; if they haven't done their allocated tasks and haven't let anyone know, it's a $10 fine. Everyone laughs when I make this suggestion, but they do take it seriously. I've never yet known anyone be fined. People get the message.

Something I share with teams which surprises them, is that team members don't have to like each other. However, they do have to respect each other. I've also noticed when working with teams, that once people start to respect the different strengths each person brings, they start to respect them and then they start to like them. We humans are so very strange.

When I work with a team, I always ensure I conduct a 1:1 with each team member in private. I ask them who on the team gives them the most stress, and they tell me.

In Chapter 2, I talked about me asking a person, 'Who in your family does this person remind you of?' This is such a vital question for all of us to ask.

Often, the person we are crediting with our stress is totally unaware that they've stirred your own personal baggage.

So for their sake, if not your own, please take a minute to work out whether you are putting your stuff onto the other person.

I now firmly believe that if we don't learn how to deal with our difficult family member, we will keep meeting that type of person again and again and again until we learn how to lay the ghost.

UNDERSTANDING PROJECTION IN TEAM MEMBERS

Projection definition: Unconscious discomfort, which can lead people to attribute their own uncomfortable feelings or impulses onto someone else to avoid having to confront them.

Once Trump became POTUS, I watched in daily horror as we witnessed him calling out people for the very things he was guilty of doing.

My first experience of projecting, long before Trump, was when working with a team of electrical engineers when a team member accused someone else of being 'negative'. Everyone went silent for a couple of seconds when several people called out, 'Neville you're the most negative person in this team'. He was shocked. He saw himself as objective. This led to all of us, me included, being more aware when Neville said anything, not that he was always right, rather that we could find workable solutions together.

At that stage I wasn't quite courageous enough to say to him, 'Are you aware that the behaviour you're upset about is the very behaviour you display?'

I chickened out.

Meet Helen

I was conducting my usual 1:1s with a brand-new team when Helen presented for her session. I could see from her face and tense body language that she absolutely didn't want to be interviewed. I'm always very clear that 1:1s are voluntary; if someone doesn't want to be interviewed, that's fine with me.

As soon as she sat down, she said, 'I don't want to be here' to which I responded, 'That's OK Helen, if you don't want to take advantage of this session, you're free to leave. It will not be held against you. This session is for you, no one will know what we talk about. I'm here for you.'

And then I waited.

My saying that to someone always causes a reaction. Very rarely do people walk out of the room. Most people are surprised by my comment and will sit for a while pondering their next move. I wait for them to think through what they want to do. I can almost hear their brains mulling over their decision:

- Should I go or should I stay?
- If I leave, will it be held against me?
- If I stay, will I be asked awkward questions?

After a few minutes of silence, I'll repeat something like, 'This session is 100% for you, Helen, and it will not be held against you if you decide not to stay', and then I wait some more.

The next question the person usually asks is, 'What's this about?' To which I reply, 'It's your hour to talk to me about anything you want to discuss, work or otherwise. The session is 100% confidential; no one other than you and I will know what we talk about.' And then I wait again.

I have never had anyone walk out after I've said that.

Back to Helen. I asked if she decided to stay, what she would like to talk about. Did she have anything she wanted to get off her chest about work or home?

And I waited.

Once Helen started talking, it was clear she had so many issues in her life it was hard to know where to start. She was upset about 'other people', how rude they were, how ungrateful, how difficult to please, how lazy, how inefficient.

Which was fascinating because her boss had told me she was one of his most grumpy employees; she was rude; ungrateful and downright lazy. One hundred per cent projection then.

I asked her to think about just one person in her life that she would like to have a conversation with about *their* 'laziness, or *their* selfishness', and it turned out she was in a gay relationship where she was the underdog. She was being treated like a doormat by her partner. She was being verbally and emotionally abused.

So we spent her hour talking about what she could say to her partner to begin standing up for herself.

I can't say Helen became an angel overnight, but her boss did comment that she seemed a lot happier when she came to work and wasn't being quite so antagonistic to her co-workers.

If you're living with a person who projects their 'stuff' onto you, rather than attacking, negating or dismissing what they are saying, try understanding that it's almost a cry for help.

It's OK to say something like, 'I'm so sorry, I didn't realise I was being … how can I do that differently for you going forward?'

This is such an ice-breaking moment for someone who projects.

I can't promise it will change their behaviours overnight, but offering a gentle approach can often create an opportunity for the person projecting to do some reflecting. Worth a try.

> 'How come every time I get stabbed in the back my fingerprints are on the blade'
> —Jerry B. Harvey

CHAPTER 4
BULLIES AT WORK

'People who love themselves don't hurt other people. The more we hate ourselves, the more we want others to suffer.'

—Dan Pearce

WHEN CONFLICT TURNS INTO BULLYING AND HARASSMENT

As a counsellor, I've worked with conflict in relationships and families; as an HR consultant, I've worked with conflict in teams.

Dealing with conflict isn't easy. It's stressful, sometimes hurtful but ultimately, will be beneficial if the various parties take responsibility for their part in the conflict.

If people in any part of your life have baggage and hidden agendas, know that you can create some ground rules for any aspect of your life.

However, if there are more sinister behaviours in play, like bullying, harassment, narcissism or sexual harassment, then a whole new level of torture ensues.

When I receive a 'Help' call from an owner, franchisor or senior manager concerned about the conflict in a particular team, department or franchise territory, I ask for stats on:

- High turnover
- High sickness rate
- History of complaints and personal grievances

If one particular team or department has a higher turnover than any other for example, then I'd want to know more about the team leader or manager because people don't leave organisations, they leave poor managers.

Then it becomes important to understand the difference between say, a poorly trained manager or franchisee; a tough manager/franchisee and a manager/franchisee who could be bullying their people. And it becomes vital to understand what bullying IS and what it isn't: what harassment is and what it isn't.

A lot of people use the term 'bully' when they're actually experiencing a tough manager, Eagles will fall into the tough manager category. They're not known to be kind, thoughtful or gentle. They're deadline and bottom-line-orientated and it frustrates the heck out of them if people are not performing to their standards.

You may be experiencing a manager who has been promoted beyond their capabilities—what's known as The Peter Principle.

Some managers are just old, tired, or terminally grumpy and negative. Although such people can be singularly awful to work with, they're not bullies.

You may even be dealing with a manager who is going through their own private issues and is on a permanently short fuse. Once again, if these are new behaviours for this particular manager, they're understandable, not welcome, not appropriate but not bullying.

What is vital though, is that in any organisation, any form of poor treatment of staff must be dealt with by the person at the top. The reputation of a business is on the line.

Yes, it takes courage and determination to deal with the perpetrators of such behaviours because bullies and harassers rarely if ever, take responsibility for their behaviours. They will never stop until they are called out.

The greater tragedy is that such people have a way of charming senior management with their amazing results, and senior staff love great results, never questioning how those results have been achieved.

So results at what cost?

WHAT BULLYING ISN'T

One of my dearest friends knew I was writing this book on bullying and called in to tell me about a very funny experience her husband had just had.

Penny and her husband own a few rental properties. Her husband is a retired engineer and a world-class handyman. He has all their properties itemized on a spreadsheet with a firm schedule for the maintenance due on each property.

Meet Jan

Jan, the husband of my friend, let one of their tenants know that he would like to call in the following week to do some routine maintenance and asked if the tenant would like to be there while he did the work. He'd met the tenant a couple of times but hadn't had any interaction with her for a while.

The tenant gave him a time and day that would be convenient and he duly arrived.

He was met by a very angry woman. The second she opened the door to him, she let him know that she did not appreciate receiving such rude emails and that she hadn't been impressed with his attitude the last time he visited. She said she found him rude and did not like being in his energy. Her final words were, 'I will not be bullied by you.'

Jan, my friend's husband, was stunned. It took him a few minutes to regain his composure. He told the tenant that he was shocked by her attack on him and told her in no uncertain terms that he's not a bully, he's DUTCH!!

We all had a chuckle about his reaction and response because Jan is very direct, and he can come across in emails as being a bit terse. His Dutch heritage coupled with being an engineer make him who he is. The Dutch, German and South African languages are very direct. I had a friend who worked in Holland for Shell and his first year there was a nightmare for him. He felt that all his Dutch colleagues spoke to him (in his opinion) like an idiot child. After a chat with a few other English oil executives he was reassured that how they were treating him was how they treated everyone.

So it's important to know what bullying isn't before we go accusing someone of such a trait.

Bullying isn't:

- Excluding someone occasionally from meetings or social gatherings
- Not liking someone. It's OK to decide someone isn't your cup of tea, it doesn't mean they are bullies, just someone you would rather not hang out with
- Someone who shouts at everyone, though not a great leadership trait, isn't bullying
- Someone who has a permanent short fuse, for whatever reason
- And it absolutely isn't someone who demands high performance from everyone
- Someone who has an abrupt way of communicating, verbally or via email with everyone

WHAT BULLYING IS

Bullying is:

- The abuse of power and position
- It is deliberate, debilitating and repeated
- It is usually targeted at one person because of their popularity, competence or vulnerability

Bullying can happen anywhere, in person or online and at any time. It can be verbal, physical or emotional. It can be obvious or covert.

Bullying behaviours can be:

- Manipulating someone to do a job they are uncomfortable doing

- Setting unreasonable deadlines
- Withholding information, raises and possible promotion
- Leaving them off important meeting notifications
- Making personal and off-colour remarks to a person in private
- Making threats, if you don't do X then I'll be forced to do Y
- Taking credit for other people's results
- Sabotaging a person in some way so they look incompetent

No matter the rationale, bullying is totally unacceptable.

Bullies tend to target people who are:

- Younger than them
- Smaller than them
- Subordinate to them
- Smarter than them
- More socially adept than them
- More popular than them

Bullying always involves behaviours like:

- Intimidating
- Insulting
- Minimizing
- Humiliating
- Threatening
- Excluding
- Spreading rumours about the target

The payoff for bullies is that it makes the target fear them. They have power over the person and can intimidate their target by doing things they would rather not do or even to set the target up for failure to make them look dumb.

THE CONFUSION BETWEEN BULLYING AND HARASSMENT

Harassment is linked to:

- Gender, colour, race
- Disability and difference
- Prejudice of some kind

The major difference, even though they can look the same is that bullying is about 'power' whereas harassment is more about public humiliation.

Sadly, some bullies are also harassers, which adds to the confusion and pain for their targets.

Bullies will usually target one person and often abuse them out of sight of other people, so it becomes at most a 'he said/she said' situation, whereas harassment is usually public and aimed at a group or sector: women or people of colour or even people with physical handicaps.

Harassers love attention, they love an audience, and they think they're funny and smart when they're neither of those things.

I've had many people tell me they're being bullied, and when I ask them to tell me how this behaviour manifests, they may say something like, 'Well he shouts at everyone and has us all walking on eggshells.'

This behaviour isn't bullying, it's terrible leadership and falls more into the category of harassing because he yells at *everyone*.

'My female boss loves calling me out at meetings and making me look stupid'. Once again, terrible leadership but falls more into the category of harassment.

'My older male boss is sweet as pie to me in front of everyone, but when I'm on my own with him he becomes a monster'. This is bullying.

Bullies do not like witnesses!

THE DIFFERENCE BETWEEN A BULLY AND A NARCISSIST

According to Psychology Today, not all narcissists are bullies, but many bullies are narcissists.

There is a thought that bullies actually do know when to stop, whereas narcissists literally have no off switch.

According to Craig Malkin, a clinical psychologist and instructor at Harvard Medical School, narcissists tend to possess a grandiose sense of self, feel entitled to special treatment and are prone to emotional outbursts.

He goes on to say that narcissists need to feed their intense insecurities and seek out constant reminders of their self-worth.

As I write this chapter, Donald Trump is in court over the alleged 'hush money' case. He has a young woman following him around with a mobile printer, printing off any favourable headlines she finds so he can look through them while he's in court, this way he can reassure himself that someone, somewhere thinks he's great.

The single most obvious sign of being a narcissist is that they demand to be treated well; to be praised; to be lorded, whilst displaying zero empathy for another human being. They are totally unable to see their own faults and will have public tantrums if anyone dares to call them out for their inappropriate behaviour and comments.

IS NARCISSISM ON THE RISE?

Because I'd become both fascinated and appalled watching Donald Trump from the day he came down the escalator, I was more alert to his behaviours showing up in other leaders.

Narcissism suddenly seemed to be everywhere I looked. Is narcissism on the rise or are we now just more aware of such awful people because of Trump?

When in doubt, ask Google.

There's been a lot of blame placed on social media for this increase in self-absorption and grandstanding and what seems like a never-ending 'me' craze.

However, researcher Shawn Bergman pointed out what Aristotle told us so many years ago, 'There's a significant amount of psychological research that shows that one's personality is fairly well-established by age seven, and given that Facebook's policy doesn't allow users to register until age 13, the personality traits of typical users are fairly well-ingrained by the time they get on a social network.'

Does the blame for the rise in narcissism then rest at home and at school? I don't think any other generation has ever been given so much praise and encouragement. I know my generation was never told we could be, do and have anything we wanted.

Schools also seem to have tapped into what I've called the 'praise craze'. Are we in danger of creating narcissists by overpraising and setting unrealistic expectations? Did the decision not to keep the score in school sports set kids up to never learn how to lose?

By setting unrealistic expectations is society creating the massive increase in mental health challenges our kids are now suffering? Are exams now set to make every student feel 'safe'?

Is this 'only winners, no losers' setting up the confusion between helping our kids build healthy self-esteem and setting them up for failure by telling them they are amazing and brilliant when perhaps they are just ordinary kids?

I believe a healthy person is equipped to deal with winning and losing. It's part of life. We really do win some and lose some.

IS THERE A POSITIVE SIDE TO NARCISSISM?

When researching narcissism and realizing that a whole lot of high-ranking managers I've worked with seem to have narcissistic tendencies, I wondered if perhaps there were any pluses to the traits.

According to psychologist Stephen Johnson, narcissists have five positive traits, but even those positive traits have a downside.

They have charm and charisma, they can be very persuasive, they are natural rule breakers, they are overachievers, and they avoid any thoughts of 'inadequacy'. In other words, they are perfect just as they are.

It would appear that the results of their five traits are mostly temporary. They talk a good talk but are not always so good at achieving the results they promise.

But worse, according to Johnson, it's all a front. He goes on to say that the narcissist 'is someone who has "buried his true self-expression in response to early injuries and replaced it with a highly developed, compensatory false self." Many narcissists behave as they do because, deep down, they feel like the "ugly duckling."'

UNDERSTANDING NARCISSISM IN MANAGEMENT

It would appear then, that narcissists are a charming version of a bully, a smiling, charming, persuasive version. The problem is, they are even more dangerous than bullies simply because they are charming and persuasive.

According to *Insights by Standford Business,* 'When the person at the top of a team or business is malignant and self-serving, unethical behaviour cascades through the organization and becomes legitimized'.

They go on to say, 'Sometimes they're as good as their promise. But many turn out to be not just confident but arrogant and entitled. Instead of being bold, they're merely impulsive'.

Narcissists lack empathy and exploit others without compunction. They ignore expert advice and treat those who differ with contempt and hostility. Above all, they demand personal loyalty.

Meet Jean

I was over the moon after applying for the job of personnel manager in a manufacturing plant. I was one of three PMs this manufacturing company had taken on at the same time. We were all interviewed by the same female HR manager, and we felt blessed that she had chosen us from many, many applicants. We all felt very special.

In our early days, Jean was amazing. We had the best support, were all sent on the most up-to-date HR training available, and all came back with different ideas as to how we could apply what we'd learned in our particular factory.

Clare had a health and safety background, so she worked on improving aspects of H & S in her area. Lara was a spreadsheet person and started a process of collating all the personnel stats in her area.

I'd been inspired by the story of the self-managing teams set up in the UK during the Second World War when men were needed to fight and coal mines were told they had to manage production with half the number of men. One mine manager in South Yorkshire set teams up without a supervisor because he simply didn't have the manpower. Not only did these teams maintain the same levels of production twice the number of men had managed, they actually doubled production, with half the number of men.

I'd taken the idea back to my South Auckland territory and we made history with the levels of production we achieved.

You'd have thought that Jean would be delighted at the strides all three of us were making in our different ways. Quite the opposite. She was furious with all three of us because we were using our initiative without her permission.

Two years after being employed, Clare and I left around the same time. I interviewed several amazing people to find my replacement and offered the job to a well-trained experienced personnel manager from another manufacturing plant from the East Coast of New Zealand.

Jean overruled my selection and put one of her secretaries into the job. A young woman with zero background, zero qualifications and after a few months in the job, zero suitability. She left.

It wasn't until several years later that I realized Jean was probably a narcissist. She certainly made my life impossible once the self-managing teams were being lauded, hence my decision to leave.

Narcissist traits:

- They are full of grandiosity and self-importance
- Have an acute need to be admired
- Have an absence of empathy
- Dismiss or devalue other people's achievements
- Have an angry reaction to anyone criticising them
- Have a desperate need for attention

In the end of course, Jean self-destructed. After Clare and I left and the secretary she chose to replace me left, and she had replaced another personnel manager with her sister, senior management turned their sights on Jean. She was asked to resign.

What a tragedy for all concerned.

HOW TO DEAL WITH A BULLY IF YOU ARE THEIR TARGET

I would highly recommend that you **never tackle a bully,** particularly if you're alone with them.

Hear them out, ask what they want you to do differently and then get out of their space.

If this is the first time they've targeted you, document everything. Write what has been said to you, done to you, how you've been treated, and document what you've been asked to do differently. Note the date and the time in your diary. Start a paper trail. This is to test if this is a one-off for all the reasons I've listed as NOT being bullying.

Unless you've been asked to do something that is unlawful or unethical, do what they've asked you to do. Let them know you've done what they asked and wait for the response.

If the person is a genuine bully, no matter what you've done it will not meet their needs, they actually weren't asking you to do something, they were testing you to see if you would make a good target. Bullies love an easy target.

If they seem to be in a very different frame of mind and are happy with whatever it was they asked you to do, then you've tested them out. They're not a bully in the traditional sense of the word, they may be just a normal person who was having a bad day.

If, however, they are a bully, they'll very likely take this second opportunity to berate you for not doing the job the way they wanted it done, because no matter how you'd done the job, for a bully it was never about the job it was always about the power they have over you.

Document the second encounter and take the issue to someone higher in the organisation to lay your concerns. Now is the time to let someone else know you suspect you are being bullied.

Be very careful who you involve at a senior level in your own organisation. I've heard so many stories of HR managers or senior managers telling the bully that a person has laid a complaint against them and the bully will literally make that person's life hell.

Meet Wendy

Wendy (a Dove) realised quite quickly that she was being bullied by her female boss, a franchisee in a very popular retail outlet employing only women.

After numerous incidents, she raised her concerns to the head office. She was told that they didn't get involved in 'operational matters' and she had to sort it out with the franchisee.

She had several doctor's appointments because of her stress levels and eventually left because of the toll this woman's treatment was having on her health.

As we speak, Wendy is working with a lawyer and taking the franchisee to court.

Given that the franchisor wanted no part of the situation, this was probably not the first time this woman had been reported. While Wendy worked for this business, she had seen several highly qualified women leave, so felt sure she wasn't the first person this person had bullied.

Until the franchisor decides to take action, Wendy probably won't be the last.

What sort of business allows this abuse to happen? If nothing else they should care about their brand image and reputation. Clearly not.

THE EFFECTS OF BULLYING

Effects can be lifelong. If you've been bullied as a child by an angry father or discontented mother, your 0–7 years will have been affected.

If you've been bullied by an older sibling, you may experience the stress and powerlessness of that for the rest of your life.

Targets may experience:

- Depression/mental health issues

- Eating disorders
- Sleeping disorders
- Hypertension
- Loneliness/anxiety
- Absenteeism
- Thoughts of suicide

Q: Why don't we tackle bullies when we see this happening to someone?

A: Because we fear we'll become the bully's next target.

WHY DO PEOPLE BULLY OTHERS?

There are a million reasons why some people feel the need to treat people so poorly:

- It may be a learned behaviour
- They may be victims of bullying at home via a parent or sibling. Feeling powerless at home, they may head to school and take their pain and powerlessness out on a smaller kid at school. Or in a work situation, the person bullying you may be being bullied by someone senior to them and so they take their pain out on someone else
- They may have worked out that bullying someone gets them what they want
- They may be feeling insecure and inadequate and berating someone smaller or more popular than them gives them a feeling of power
- They may have low self-esteem
- They may just be unhappy, miserable people and hurting someone else gives them a perverted pleasure

EFFECTS ON THE BULLY

It's easy to think there are zero effects on the bully, after all, they are the ones who are dishing out all the terror, but there are many effects on the bully:

- An increased risk of substance abuse (alcohol in particular)
- Anxiety and fear. They too could be on edge, fearing that they will be found out or challenged or even fired

CAN BULLIES CHANGE THEIR DESTRUCTIVE BEHAVIOUR?

Sadly, people with such a sad personality disorder rarely self-reflect. It's a little like the lightbulb joke, 'How many psychiatrists does it take to change a lightbulb? One, but the lightbulb has to want to change.'

It also raises the thought that people change when they see the light or when they feel the heat. If a bully is repeatedly fired for his/her behaviour, they may see the light and realise they have issues and ask for help or seek counselling, OR they can decide they are not the problem, keep doing what they've always done and find someone else to blame and a new target.

Awareness is the first step. By being aware that they keep repeating their own self-destructive behaviours, they may decide to get help. They could start a journal and take daily notes:

- What did I do today that hurt someone?
- Why did I do that?
- What could I have done differently?

They could seek counselling and be willing to talk about:

- Their childhood
- Their 0–7 years
- Their family of origin
- How they were bullied and by whom
- How that made them feel
- How they reacted
- How they took their pain out on someone else
- How they chose that particular person
- Their willingness to make amends and apologise to the person for the damage they've caused

If they're serious about changing their behaviours, they could ensure they don't fall back into their bullying ways by:

- Finding a mentor
- Making a daily promise not to hurt anyone today
- Surrounding themselves with positive people
- Finding ways to feel good about themselves
- Building their own healthy self-esteem

> 'Controllers, abusers and manipulative people don't question themselves. They don't ask themselves if the problem is them. They always say the problem is someone else.'
> —Darlene Ouimet

UNDERSTANDING AND DEALING WITH SEXUAL HARASSMENT

When people are the victim of sexual harassment, the pressure on the target can be terrifying.

Sadly, a lot of older men think that 'teasing' women about their shape or size or making off-colour jokes or suggestive remarks in front of them is funny; it isn't. Their attitude will be 'Can't you take a joke?' Such behaviour is wholly inappropriate and should never be tolerated in a work situation.

The entire #MeToo movement came about because of Harvey Weinstein's demanding sexual favours in order for female actresses to be considered for movie selection. The inappropriate behaviour could be:

- Verbal (making suggestive comments)
- Visual (showing someone off colour pictures)
- Physical (touching without permission)

Sexual harassment will have the same outcomes as bullying, the target will perform poorly, be anxious, stressed and will take a lot of time off work.

> *'If your flirting strategy is indistinguishable from harassment, it's not everyone else that's the problem.'*
> —John Scalzi

DEALING WITH ONLINE BULLYING

Cyberbullying is insidious. You can't see the person, you can't deal with the person face to face, and they're usually anonymous. You feel utterly powerless.

Technology has created some amazing opportunities for all of us. We can Google just about anything we want to know on any topic. We can communicate with people we would never meet from different countries, different cultures, different levels of expertise on a million different topics.

The downside is that we often give away too much information about ourselves and can leave ourselves open to all manner of inappropriate communication.

All forms of social media are an opportunity for someone with a grudge to attack us.

I'm no longer on Facebook.

I'd written *Lessons in Leadership: 50 Ways to Avoid Falling into the Trump Trap*, calling out his appalling leadership traits. Given that I worked in the corporate arena, I felt sure there would be certain types of managers who would look at him and think that this is what a great leader does. It absolutely isn't.

I was building a following on Facebook as a result of the book and was calling out what Trump was doing in the hope that people reading my comments would realise that what he was doing was not great leadership and not make the same mistakes.

Some unknown person took exception. They reported me for abuse (I was never abusive) and my page was shut down with no notice and no information as to why I'd been shut down.

However, whoever this person was, they clearly were clever with technology because they started creating ads on Facebook in my name and charging my bank account for them!

I was locked out of my account on a Friday, and the very next day watched money being taken out of my PayPal account. This happened over the weekend when traditional banks were closed. I contacted PayPal, but they didn't want to know! By Monday morning the phantom person had run up over $2000 worth of debt.

There was no way to find out who was doing this. Once you're blocked on Facebook, there's no helpdesk, no one to call, and no one to tell you how to get back onto the site. I had just lost 10,000 followers.

I was waiting for my bank to open first thing Monday morning to lay a complaint about whoever it was that was taking money out of my account. Fortunately, the bank could see I had no record of ever purchasing advertising on Facebook so they were happy to organize the money to be returned to me. In full.

Once I'd stopped the money drain, I got really angry with Facebook. They'd cancelled my account, given me no warning, no reason why and no information as to how I could get back on. Yet they were still letting someone continue purchasing advertising in my name.

Pretty unethical in my book.

So if you use any form of social media be careful.

- Check your accounts regularly
- Check your bank accounts every day
- If someone starts abusing you, don't bother engaging with them, just block them
- Do not send money to anyone on social media, there are so many scams around and some of them are very slick
- Be careful what photos you put on social media, particularly of your children

If you're being abused or fleeced, you can usually contact the platform administrators (with the exception of Facebook and PayPal it seems).

If the threats are serious enough to have you concerned for your safety, you can report them to the police.

If you're not sure how to report someone for abusive or threatening messages, check the resources available in your own country for reporting cyberbullying.

*'If you're insulting people on the internet,
you must be ugly on the inside.'*
—Phil Lester

CHAPTER 5
STRATEGIES FOR DEALING WITH BULLYING AT HOME

'No one can make you feel inferior without your consent.'

—Eleanor Roosevelt

DELAY TACTICS WE FALL PREY TO

We're all human, most of us are nice people. We're people who wouldn't dream of being nasty or abusive to someone else, so when someone dishes out that sort of treatment to us, we tend to make excuses for them because the thought of dealing with the behaviour can be too terrifying.

Over the years of counselling, I've met parents being bullied by their children; and adult children being manipulated by their elderly parents. I've seen brother turn on brother and sister turn on sister. I've heard of neighbours tormenting neighbours and shopkeepers cheating customers. Tragically I've counselled many families where elderly parents are being bullied by their adult children and even grandchildren.

Money seems to be a bone of contention in so many relationships. Families fighting over inheritances; couples fighting over who earns more; friendships destroyed because one person borrowed money from the other and never paid it back.

There isn't much that humans won't do to abuse or torment another human if they're that way inclined.

Denial: There's no problem here, everything is fine

Avoidance: I know there's a problem but I'm not up to dealing with it so I'll just keep avoiding the person or the problem. Busy being busy is a classic avoidance technique.

Abdication: It's nothing to do with me, I'm going to keep right out of this situation, I don't want a bar of what's going on

Excuses:

- He/she is having a tough time at work so he/she has to be able to vent somewhere and if they can't vent at home where can he/she vent?
- It's just a stage he/she is going through
- He/she has just had some bad luck
- He/she is facing some health issues

Denying there's a problem or making excuses for poor behaviour or being so busy you don't have time to attend to something won't make the problem go away, but it will make us delude ourselves that there isn't a problem in the first place so why are other people stressing?

'Denial is not a river in Egypt'
—Alcoholics Anonymous

NAMING THE GAME

When I'm working 1:1 with someone for the first time, I ask them to tell me what their problem is, and I get fascinating responses like:

- My husband is a psycho (meaning psychopath) or
- My wife is a sociopath or
- My mother is a pure narcissist

Unless we are professional psychologists, these are all terms we really shouldn't use. Mostly because we probably don't have a single clue as to what they mean.

Definitions

A psycho (psychopath) describes a set of personality traits and behaviours frequently associated with a lack of emotional sensitivity and empathy, impulsivity, superficial charm and insensitivity to punishing consequences. 'Psychopathy is observed in about 1% of the population, is much more prevalent in men than women, and affects about 15–25% of the prison population.'

A sociopath will display 'a profound lack of conscience—a flaw in the moral compass that typically steers people away from breaking common rules and toward treating others decently. This disconnect, however, may be hidden by a charming demeanour.'

A narcissist will display 'a grandiose sense of self-importance, a lack of empathy for others, a need for excessive admiration and the belief that they are unique and deserving of special treatment.'

Rather than get into using derogatory 'names' I prefer to ask the person I'm working with to explain the 'behaviours' the other person is displaying that makes them think they're a narcissist or whatever name they've ascribed to the person.

Usually, they'll say things like:

- He treats me like a doormat
- She needs to know where I am every second of the day
- My mother thinks I'm her personal banker

And so we start to work on the behaviours the person is displaying rather than getting caught up in 'name calling'.

When working with women's groups, I'll make cards containing the words and phrases below. I ask that this be a silent exercise as I put the cards in the centre of the table. I then ask participants to choose the card/s that best represents how they're being treated by someone in their life.

Words like teasing, taunting, isolating, twisting my words, blaming me for things they did, minimizing.

This is such a traumatic exercise for attendees when they choose one, two or even three of the cards. It's an incredibly emotional exercise, but it's also a vital exercise. It's a person's moment of truth as they see and acknowledge the treatment they're receiving at someone's hands.

It's what I call 'naming the game'.

And then I give the attendees the definitions of each of the behaviours as a handout.

Definitions

Teasing can simply be a playful act between siblings, partners or work colleagues. It becomes harmful when the teasing becomes personal or off colour and if the intention is to deliberately make the target feel uncomfortable.

Tormenting is the next level of teasing, it's when the person being tormented says 'This is not OK' or 'These comments are not funny and cross a line'. The intention of tormenting someone is to make them feel uncomfortable and miserable.

Minimizing is when a person makes you feel 'less than' or dumb or stupid. It is absolutely designed to belittle the target.

Sarcasm is when someone says one thing but means the opposite i.e. 'You're so smart', meaning, you're so dumb. Sarcasm is used to insult someone, berate them and put them down.

Neglect is when a parent or significant other in your life simply pays you no attention. It could be not providing food, warmth or emotional support.

Blaming is the intentional act of putting the responsibility for something one person did onto another person.

Controlling happens when a person tries to make the other person conform to what they want that person to do. It's an insidious form of manipulation, particularly if threats are used. 'If you don't do X then I will do Y'.

Isolating is the deliberate attempt to cut a person off from information or people.

Twisting is the act of repeating a person's words back to them inaccurately to make that person feel confused or stupid.

Gas lighting is when one person makes another person doubt their memory or perception of an event.

Projecting is when a person puts their issues onto another person as if they caused a problem or behaved a certain way.

Triangulation is a tactic where one person complains to a third party in the hope that the third party will tell you what they're upset about or what they want you to do differently.

Manipulation can come in many forms and is designed to keep another person off balance through making hints or veiled threats about abandonment, infidelity, or rejection.

The victim card is played when people who have done everything they can to get you to do something you don't want to do and nothing has worked, so they will bring out their 'poor me' card. The aim is to make you feel sorry for them and to do what they've been trying to pressure you into doing. Mothers, children and teens are particularly good at this game.

Harassing is when a person uses words or behaviours that threaten, intimidate or demean another person. It is behaviour that is unwanted, uninvited, and unwelcome and deliberately causes distress to the target.

Abusing is next level up from all the previous forms of manipulation I've mentioned so far. It's when the person takes on a more dangerous form of attempting to get you to bend to their will. This is when the mental health and emotional well-being of the target will be affected.

Bullying is deliberate. It involves a misuse of power. It is rarely a one-off situation. It is intended to subjugate the target: to make them so terrified of the perpetrator that they'll do whatever they're told.

Once attendees have selected the behaviours that are affecting them, I ask them to take the following reality test.

EXERCISE: DEFINE WHAT AND WHO

As you've read all these definitions, you may be experiencing one or two of the seemingly less threatening of the behaviours or you may be experiencing a whole raft of them in your life, your family, your closest friends or your significant relationship.

Other than harmless teasing, all the behaviours mentioned on the cards are NOT OK.

Complete the questions below, it may be that the same name appears in most or even all of the spaces, but it may be that you have several people who are not treating you kindly:

1. Who in your life teases you beyond what is pleasant or funny?

....

2. Who has turned teasing into a form of torment despite you asking them to stop?

....

3. Who in your life minimises you and tries to make you feel small and insignificant?

....

4. Who in your life uses sarcasm to make you feel stupid?

....

5. Who in your life neglected you when you were small?

....

6. Who in your life neglects you now?

....

7. Who is quick to blame you for something you know both know they did?

....

8. Who in your life tries to control you: to pressure you into doing what they want you to do even knowing that you don't want to do what they're asking?

....

9. Who in your life did or does isolate you; forgets to let you know about meetings at work or family/social gatherings?

....

10. Who twists what you say to try to make you feel unsettled?

....

11. Who in your life gaslights you—gets you second-guessing yourself?

....

12. Who in your life projects their baggage onto you?

....

13. Who in your life never tells you directly something you are doing they don't like but gets someone else to tell you (triangulation)?

....

14. Who in your life plays the victim card when you refuse to do something for them?

....

15. Who in your life will deliberately harass you into doing their bidding?

....

16. Who in your life do you believe is abusing you, either emotionally, sexually, financially or physically?

....

17. Who in your life has bullied you or IS bullying you?

....

ACKNOWLEDGE THE PATTERNS YOU'VE ALLOWED TO OCCUR

It's really tough to acknowledge your own part in what's happening with the difficult people in your life. But you do have a part to play. It's so much easier to think the problem is the other person, but it really does take two to tango.

- How long has this situation been going on?
- Have you tried to discuss how you feel?
- If you have, what was the outcome?
- How do things stand now?

I've had many women say that they've tried to raise the subject of whatever it is they having challenges with and have either been ignored, laughed at for being so petty, or shouted at for being so rude. And so they give up. And so, the person will keep doing what they've always done because we've now rolled over.

Only you can change the situation. If you were ignored the first time, the second and even the tenth time, keep at it. Keep saying 'This isn't OK and I need you to stop …'

You may even have to consider stating some consequences if the situation is serious enough.

For example, if your problem has been a teenage son or daughter regularly taking the car and leaving it on empty. This means that when you need the car to get to work the car is on empty and you are now going to be late for work.

The consequence has to be, 'Unless you top the car up next time you use it, then I'll no longer let you use my car'. And you must stick to that consequence. Don't waver. Kids can wear us down so easily.

IS YOUR SIGNIFICANT OTHER A BULLY? A TEST.

You may be in a relationship with someone you fear is a bully, but you're not quite sure. This list of questions isn't proof, but it is an indication—so tread warily if it has confirmed your worst fears.

Does he/she:

- Keep upsetting you even when you've asked numerous times for him/her to stop? Y/N
- Get aggressive if you call them out or give them negative feedback? Y/N
- Verbally abuse you on a regular basis? Y/N
- Keep you short of money and expect you to account for every cent you spend? Y/N
- Isolate you from friends and family? Y/N
- Control you by making threats against you, your family, your pets if you don't do what they tell you to do? Y/N
- Show signs of being excessively possessive? Y/N
- Make off-colour remarks about you in front of other people? Y/N
- Become jealous if you talk to a member of the opposite sex? Y/N
- Make you walk on eggshells if you upset them? Y/N
- Become unpredictable/agitated if you don't do what they want you to do? Y/N
- Pressure you into doing things they know you don't like doing? Y/N
- Blames you for things they did? Y/N
- Tell you what to wear or gets upset if what you wear is likely to draw attention to you? Y/N
- Hold grudges? Y/N
- Keep you from seeing friends and/or family? Y/N

All of the above behaviours are signs that your significant other is a 'controller/abuser'. In the beginning of your relationship, the person will tell you he/she is doing this because they love you so much and they just want to protect you. Protect you from whom though?

These behaviours don't get better with time, they will get worse. Controlling people are deeply insecure and they will take their insecurities out on you. They will tell you that 'If only you would … they wouldn't have to keep on at you'. The problem is that no matter what you do or how much you bend yourself out of shape to please them, you'll never please them. They're the ones with the problem, not you.

Remember I shared my own story of getting into that abusive relationship; a relationship that was a mirror image of how I had been treated by my stepfather.

By the time I met the man I'd had years of counselling, I thought I was sorted, that I was now a strong woman. Within a very short space of time, I was a dithering mess. I would use my assertiveness training and ask him not to do certain things because they were incredibly upsetting.

He had a pattern of behaviour that progressed this way:

1. He would say, 'I know I have issues and I don't want to lose you, I will do everything in my power to change'.
2. Within a week or so that would change to 'WE have problems, and I'm willing to work with you to keep our relationship strong'.
3. Within another week or so, the dialogue would become 'You have issues, Ann. YOU need help.'

We made numerous appointments to see a relationship counsellor, and he would always back out.

'An abuser can seem emotionally needy. You can get caught in a

trap of catering to him, trying to fill a bottomless pit. But he's not so much needy as entitled, so no matter how much you give him, it will never be enough. He will just keep coming up with more demands because he believes his needs are your responsibility until you feel drained down to nothing.'

—Lundy Bancroft

LEARNING TO STAND YOUR GROUND

Learning to stand up to people who aren't treating you well, teenagers, family, co-workers or bosses, is not easy. It's scary and in some cases it can be terrifying.

When I'm working with my teams and women's groups, I suggest that if they are fearful of standing up to someone at work, that they practice their new assertiveness techniques on someone at home, and vice versa.

It is critical that before anyone confronts another person with their 'phrase' they practice it over and over again with a trusted friend or relative. The more times we use our 'phrase', the more natural it becomes and the more confident we feel about stating our case.

Choose an easy challenge first. Set yourself up for success.

Step 1: Choose the person you're going to elect to speak to and decide whether it's a home situation or a work situation.

Step 2. A work scenario. Decide what the behaviour is that you find unacceptable (be really clear what the behaviour is), i.e. talking over you at meetings or making fun of you in front of your work colleagues. Name the game. Leave no room for ambiguity.

Step 3. Practice your statement several times with your friend and ask them to be realistic in their responses. When you confront the actual person, they will react in some shape or form. You need to be prepared for every and all possible reactions.

Your statement needs to be something like, 'John, I have difficulty when you talk over me in meetings, and I'd like you not to do that going forward. Do you understand why I find that upsetting?'

Asking a yes/no question at the end of your chosen phrase is deliberate, it gives the person pause before they reply. By asking a closed question, you are halfway to diffusing a potential argument.

Wait for the reaction when you confront John. Please talk to the person in private. You'll get a whole lot better reaction if you speak quietly and in private than if you accost him in front of your co-workers. Hopefully, John will be apologetic and give you permission to check him if he does it again. However, he may not be happy with you calling him out and may want to argue.

A home scenario: Mary (sister) 'I have difficulty when you expect me to do all the running around for our mother when you know I have three children to ferry around after school. I need you to take a turn now and again to get her to her doctor's appointment. Can we set a schedule for doing that?' Another yes/no response.

Once again, hopefully, Mary will be apologetic and happy to work out a roster, however, if she wants to turn the conversation into an argument, I'll show you how to deal with that shortly also.

The main thing at this stage of learning to stand your ground is to be clear about who the problem person is and what the actual behaviour is that's causing you to be upset. Don't waffle.

WARNING. Never put yourself in a dangerous situation, if the person you are considering confronting is likely to react violently, DO NOT CONFRONT THEM.

REACTIONS TO YOU STANDING YOUR GROUND

There will be reactions. Plan ahead for possible reactions. Consider using the DOPE personalities as a guide for how this person is likely to react.

- Surprise. The person had no idea that they were upsetting you. (This could be a reaction from any of the profiles)
- Arguing/denial. 'No I don't' (Peacock/Eagle)
- Attack. 'How dare you, who do you think you are?' (Eagle/Peacock?)
- Silent treatment. In this scenario, it isn't unusual for the person to simply walk away and give you the silent treatment for hours, days and even weeks. In families the silent treatment can last years and even generations. (Owl/Dove?)
- Blame. 'I don't do that, you're the one who does that.' (Peacock/Eagle?)
- Tears. 'I can't believe you would treat me like this.' (Dove)
- Fogging. This is a defence mechanism people use when confronted. They hear you out and literally change the subject. Fogging is a denial technique. You may have caught them by surprise and the person becomes defensive and does anything they can not to deal with the topic. (Any of the profiles.)

'Overcoming abuse doesn't just happen. It takes positive steps every day. Let today be the day you start to move forward.'
—Assunta Hannis

SOME BASIC TECHNIQUES FOR DEALING WITH REACTIONS

Many years ago, I was knee-deep in a particularly challenging situation with a close friend. I wanted to deal with the situation without risking our very special friendship. Fortunately, I discovered an amazing book *When I Say No I Feel Guilty* by Manuel Smith. I read the book again and again and again. I'm a Dove remember, and at that stage of my life, not the most assertive person in the world. My friend is a red-haired Peacock. Quite terrifying when roused!

The book recommends:

- **Using I statements, not You statements**. By saying, 'I'm having challenges with xyz', rather than, 'You really annoy me when you do xyz' you have a far better chance of having an adult conversation rather than risking a red-haired flare-up. By saying 'I' you are owning the conversation whereas by saying 'You' you're metaphorically pointing a finger at the other person.
- **The power of the pause**. When you've made your statement, calmly and softly, shut up. Wait for the reaction, keep breathing. Don't rush to fill the silence.
- Once the person has reacted, and they will react in some way, wait for a break in the conversation, hear them out, they may have a reason for what they're doing. Once you've listened to their point of view, the next step is to look for **Workable Compromises**. 'So if you could perhaps ….., then I think that would work really well for both of us'?
- **The broken record technique**. Some people will have strong reactions and may have several creative ways to tell you that you're wrong, that you misunderstood them, that

you are being overly sensitive. Hear them out, Use your 'pause' technique, Once they start running out of excuses or attempts at denying there's a problem, step in with your 'phrase' again. The strategy in this situation is to repeat the same phrase in a calm way until the other person realises you are not going to be side-tracked.

- **Working out whose monkey it is.** The 'monkey' strategy simply asks that you work out whose 'problem' this is. If it's a friend borrowing money or that person talking over you in meetings, it is *their* problem, *their* monkey, you are simply asking them to do something differently and stating why what they are doing is upsetting to you.
- **Not negotiable.** It's important when having these discussions that you know what your bottom line is; what you are willing to negotiate and what you absolutely will not negotiate. **Sound back** what you've just heard. 'I'd like to check that I understand your point of view'. Something along the lines of 'So you believe that I'm being oversensitive?' A closed question. If they say yes, then your response needs to be your phrase again with an acknowledgement of what they've just said, 'I hear you saying that you think I'm being oversensitive, however, from where I stand, what you're doing is upsetting me, and I'm asking you to be aware of what you are doing, and to consider not doing it. Could that work for you?' Closed questions.

It takes a pretty insensitive person to hear you out and then ignore what you're asking. Sadly, there are some people who will do exactly that—ignore what you are saying!

THE POWER OF HAND GESTURES

I teach men and women these two powerful hand gestures. The one-handed gesture is really useful if someone is invading your space. The one-handed gesture signals that you want the other person to 'stop right there'; either physically or verbally. This creates a space where you can make a request 'Can I stop you there, I'm feeling…………..when you……………and what I'd like you to do is……………'

You'll need to fill in the gaps here to reflect the problem you are having.

Practice writing down what you'd like to say if you have someone who regularly steps into your space or who over-talks you or literally 'gets into your face'.

Consequences: The two-handed gesture is even more forceful. It really does say, stop right there. This may be your last-ditch stand after all other conversations you've had with the person have failed. If you've had numerous conversations of the please stop variety, and none of them have worked; if you've tried your one-handed gesture and still the person isn't listening, then it is absolutely OK to use the two-handed gesture and raise your voice just slightly. Up until this point, I've always stressed speaking softly, but clearly what you've been doing isn't working so now we need to step up the forcefulness with the big gun of the two-handed gesture.

Repeat your phrase more forcefully. If your situation has reached this stage, you may need to hand out a consequence. This conversation will go along these lines:

'Martin, I've asked you several times to stop putting me down in meetings. I've explained how upsetting that is and clearly, you have no intention of ceasing doing that. If you continue doing that in meetings, I will report you. Do you understand what I'm now saying?' Closed question. Shut up. Wait the person out. Maintain eye contact.

It really does take an incredibly arrogant or ignorant person to ignore you at this stage. If they say 'No, I don't agree with you and you can do your darndest, I really don't care' then you must see the consequence through, you must report the person to someone in authority.

WHAT TO SAY, WHEN TO SAY IT AND HOW TO SAY IT

DEALING WITH A TRICKY WORK SITUATION

Please remember that I'm a Dove, so the responses I'm offering here come from that perspective. I hope they'll still work for you.

James and Ella attend the same quality control meetings and whenever Ella puts forward ideas or asks questions, James immediately cuts her off and speaks over her.

Ella's phrase, 'James I wonder if you're aware that you consistently speak over me at meetings and I'm finding that hard to understand?'

Reactions

Surprise: I can see this has surprised you James so please give me your thoughts. Are you aware that you do this? A yes/no opportunity.

If James says yes, then repeat your phrase, 'So you are aware that you talk over me in meetings? Can I ask why you do that?' (And then shut up)

This gives you both an opportunity to discuss openly and honestly what goes on between you both.

In a work situation, James may be an Eagle and Ella may be a Dove. He wants to get a move on in the meeting, Ella may want to mull something over and discuss ideas with other team members at the meeting.

If the person says no, I'm not aware I do that, then 'From where I stand, that's what happens' is a great next line. 'Can you see this from my point of view?' is the follow-up question. Another yes/no opportunity.

If you get another no, then you need to leave the conversation with a calm, closing statement. Something like, 'I'm sad that you don't understand what I'm trying to tell you, so all I can do is leave my concern with you and ask that you give it some thought. I enjoy working with you and I really want to find a solution. Let's see what happens in the next meeting?'

And then walk away having left the problem with James whilst ending on a positive note but having put a marker in the ground for the next meeting.

NB: It's important to note here that if you ask a person 3 times to stop doing something that upsets you, they will never hear you and will never change, in which case you may have to make some decisions as to what you do next.

Is the job worth fighting for; can you ask for a transfer, can you accept that James is never going to hear your concerns and that you're going to have to live with the situation if you love your job?

Arguing/denial: 'No I don't' usually causes us to get into the circular argument of 'Yes you do' which gets the parties nowhere.

A better rejoinder is to say, 'From where I stand that's how it seems'. Then ask a question which will break the 'No I don't/Yes you do' cycle. Something like 'Can you see this from my standpoint?' The yes/no question again.

If yes, work towards a solution, if no, follow the next step under 'surprise' and leave the conversation with a calm, closing statement.

'I'm sad that you don't get what I'm trying to tell you, so all I can do is leave my concern with you and ask that you give it some thought. I enjoy working with you and I really want to find a solution. Let's see what happens in the next meeting?'

Attack: Stand your ground, take a deep breath and step back if you need to, it's appropriate to use your one-hand gesture if you are under attack.

Let the person wind down. Apply '**The power of the pause**'. Once the person has run out of steam, use a neutral statement along the lines of 'I haven't raised this issue to upset you, James, I've raised it because I find it upsetting when you talk over me. Can you see this from my point of view'. Yes/no.

By now I'm hoping you will be seeing the pattern of dealing with any reaction is pretty much the same.

The main thing throughout these potentially fraught conversations is to stay calm, keep breathing, keep saying your phrase in your mind until you get an opportunity to break back into the conversation.

> '*Manipulation is when someone blames you*
> *for your reaction to their disrespect.*'
> —John Jodka

HANDLING A TENSE FAMILY SITUATION

Dealing with a family member can take on a whole new level of fear and discomfort. I'm not saying the following reactions don't happen at work, but the strategies for dealing with family/close relationships are slightly different from those we use in a work situation.

I'll use an example of a family member borrowing money, an issue that is raised regularly at my women's groups.

Your phrase could be 'Mum I'm really concerned about the amount of money you've borrowed off me recently with no conversation about how you plan to pay the money back, can we talk about that?'

Expect the same reactions as we witnessed with a team member:

Silent treatment: My advice when someone is giving another person the silent treatment is to leave things a while after you've told them what you're upset about. Give them time to respond, if their response is to walk away and then give you the silent treatment, Leave things for a little while.

They may call you back to apologize or to ask meet again to talk things over. If not, take the initiative and contact the person again to see if they would like to grab a coffee. It's very rare that a person never wants to see or hear from you again. If this is the first time you've ever stood up to a significant other, their silence may be registering their shock and even embarrassment.

Some people can carry on the silent treatment for a very long time. Depending on the importance of the relationship you will need to plan how you handle the next stage of the conversation.

I'm using the example of your mum, but you may be having challenges with a sibling, a son or daughter, an aunt or uncle or even someone you've been friends with for years.

Is the relationship worth fighting for?

Obviously, you don't want to permanently fall out with your mum, but if this is a close friend, decide if it is the friendship of value to you or is it a relationship where you are the giver and your friend is the never-ending taker, and if so, do you want to continue the friendship?

Blame: This is such a 'family' strategy. If you stand up to your mother, a likely reaction is, 'You're just like your father'; or a sister saying, 'You've always been a selfish person.'

Dealing with family conflict raises a more emotional layer of concern because they matter more in your life. Work colleagues come and go, and you can always leave a job if someone isn't treating you well, but we're stuck with our families.

Tears: I can see you're upset, and I haven't raised this issue to make you feel bad, I've raised it because it's important to me that we find a solution. Do you get that? Yes/no.

Sit quietly until the person stops crying. Then make your statement again. 'I need to get this sorted because it's causing me challenges. Do you understand that?' Yes/no response.

Yes. Let's see if we can find a workable compromise so you can pay me back at an amount that's comfortable. Will that work for you? Yes/no.

If you are getting 'no' responses, then you will have to be a bit tougher if this is a financial situation.

The next phrase is along the lines of 'I understand you've had some financial challenges, but I can't keep loaning you money, it's causing significant stress for me. How about I help you work out a payment structure that chips away at what you owe me without leaving you short? How does that sound?' Yes/no.

I'm using a financial situation here because it is one of the most emotive problems between people. Someone borrowing money and making no effort to pay it back can cause the lender massive stress and worry, particularly if loaning that money has put them in a difficult financial situation.

The bottom line technique. The vital thing at this point is that you state, 'I'm sorry that things have been tough for you, but I cannot loan you any more money.' And then don't say another word. Wait until the person reacts.

Whatever the situation you're dealing with and without being threatening, your statement has to include the suggestion that you've had enough.

The final reaction and the one that takes immense patience to deal with, is when you are raising an issue with a person and they simply keep going off at tangents; changing the subject; talking about other things that have zero relevance never, ever acknowledging the problem you've raised with them.

Fogging is another fear or face-saving strategy. But there's a wonderful counter strategy for this and it's called 'broken record'.

If the person you're speaking to keeps going off at tangents, the strategy to counteract that is to repeat the same phrase over and over until they get it, you're not going to be taken off track.

'I realise this conversation is tricky for both of us, but we have to find a solution to your borrowing money off me. Do you get that?' Yes/no.

'I get it that you've had a lot of expense lately, and I understand the stress that has put you under, but we have to find a solution to your borrowing money off me. Do you see my predicament?' Yes/no.

I make no promises that having a conversation with the person you are having challenges with will create an instant miracle. But having made your statement, the person now knows you are not happy.

If you need to have several conversations before the person gets it, then so be it. Have several conversations. I can promise you each one gets easier because now you are coming from a position of 'don't mess with me' and people will get that.

NEUTRAL PHRASES THAT NO ONE CAN ARGUE WITH

You can go round in circles with so many of these discussions, so at some stage you have to stand your ground by learning to 'shut up'. I absolutely love teaching the 'shut up' strategy. Women love it. It is such an empowering strategy.

In response to their response, you could say, 'That's interesting' then shut up.

Or you could say, 'That's not how I see things' then shut up.

You could introduce a question, 'Tell me how you see things, cos I could be wrong, and if I am I'm happy to apologise?' And then shut up.

Or you could use your bottom-line strategy: 'I'd love to help, but I can't right now, sorry.' Then shut up.

Finding Workable Compromises

Once you've mastered the delicate art of 'shutting up' the other person will fill the silence. They may react negatively of course, but they may also give you an opening to offer a workable compromise, something like:

'I can't do that for you right now, but I could possibly help you in some way next week. I'll get back to you after I've checked my diary. Does that work for you?'

You could pass finding the solution over to the other person, 'I understand you have a lot going on and I don't want to let you down, what are some of your thoughts on where we go from here?'

THE *TOUGHLOVE* STRATEGY FOR DEALING WITH CONFLICT

There came a time when my children swapped personalities. My son had been my challenge when he was a child, my daughter became my nightmare when she hit the teen years.

Before I became a solo mum, my ex-husband had always been the discipline. I now had to be the person who said 'No, you can't do that' to my daughter, and that became a red rag to a bull.

My daughter literally ignored me. She started staying out way too late; she appeared to be mixing with people I felt were way too dangerous, and overnight it seemed I'd lost my easy-going daughter.

The situation between us became so tense I decided to attend a Toughlove meeting to better understand parenting a teenager who to me, seemed totally out of control.

I ended up running the local meetings with the guidance counsellor of a local boy's high school and learned so much about how to live with wayward teenagers.

Toughlove groups are simply groups of parents helping other parents try to turn the negative behaviours of teens into more positive outcomes. There are no experts in the group, the only reason you can join a group or run a group is if you have a teenager who is acting out.

The weekly sessions were simple and affirming. It was a massive relief to know that you weren't alone with the dramas you were trying to deal with.

STRATEGIES FOR DEALING WITH BULLYING AT HOME

Each week, parents started the evening's session in groups of six or seven. Every parent would have a few minutes to 'check in' to let the other parents know how their week had gone, for better or worse.

We would then move into a larger group to listen to a speaker, someone who *was* an expert on an aspect of teen behaviour, and finally, we would return to our small groups to set ourselves some homework. Every week we would declare 'one thing we would do differently this week to deal with our teen'.

The best advice we were given via the Toughlove training was that if you were the person who normally dished out the rules or discipline, for one week you did NOT do that; your significant other took that role.

In my case of course, as with a lot of the parents, we were now flying solo, so all we could do was:

- Set some boundaries
- Set the consequences for those boundaries being ignored

Simple, not necessarily easy and often quite a terrifying prospect because there was an expectation of accountability. If you had set a consequence, you were expected to implement it. No chickening out, otherwise all credibility would be lost with your teen.

For the sole parents, we were encouraged to bring in another parent to support us while we set the boundaries and the consequences if we felt the need. There was something about having another adult with you that not only helped you the parent, but really brought it home to the teen that this was a serious conversation.

'One day when your teen is grown, they really will thank you for

setting limits, giving them responsibility, having high expectations, and saying "no". Have faith in that fact. Don't sacrifice your teen's tomorrows for a more peaceful today.'

—Heather Ambrose

LEARN TO FIGHT FAIRLY

Firstly, let me share strategies that don't work if you are trying to let someone know that they are upsetting you.

Whining doesn't work.

Nagging doesn't work.

Humiliating someone in front of others doesn't work.

Comparing (if only you were more like your brother/sister/cousin/aunt) doesn't work.

All that does is make the 'nagger' even more miserable because nagging the person clearly isn't working, and it makes the poor person on the receiving end of nagging frustrated, sad, uncomfortable and miserable.

If you've read the strategies above and realized that you do one of them or several of them or even all of them. Please stop. They will never work.

So when you're planning your difficult conversation with whoever you've been nagging, create some ground rules for yourself, these will tide you over if things start to get heated.

Things like:

- I will state my case clearly and calmly

- I will ask the other person to tell me their side of the situation
- I will listen and hear what they're saying
- If I need to sound back what they've just said, then I will
- I won't interrupt them while they are talking
- If they get upset, I will stay calm
- I won't take their criticism personally, I realise what I'm saying to them may be hurtful or even a complete surprise
- I will give them time to consider what I'm saying, and if this means some time out, that's OK
- However, I will not let them negate what I'm saying. I will use my broken record technique as many times as I need to
- I don't have to be right, but I won't be made wrong
- I will not name-call or swear at the person no matter how antsy they get
- I will not storm out of the room
- I will own the problem

When we have these difficult conversations, we absolutely need to listen and hear the other person's point of view. You may learn something. You could be wrong.

Ask questions. Acknowledge that you may be wrong. This will neutralise the emotion in the conversation and will give you a break from talking and encourage the other party to put forward how the situation looks to them.

> *'God grant me the serenity to accept the things I cannot change; the courage to change the things I can and the wisdom to know the difference.'*
> —The Alcoholic's Prayer

DECIDING TO TRY A DIFFERENT STRATEGY

If what you've tried in the past to persuade someone to treat you differently hasn't worked, try a different tactic.

Meet Anita

Anita was the youngest of four sisters. Her three older sisters had been born within a few years of each other and then there was the gap of around eight years before Anita was born.

Because of the age gap, mostly her sisters ignored her and so she spent her entire childhood trying to get them to notice her and be her friend. She discovered the only way to do that was to 'gift' them something or do something for them.

Being big sisters, they revelled in this little person bending herself inside out to please them and encouraged it every step of the way, not realizing how damaging this would be to this little girl as she grew into adulthood.

Trying to people please became the pattern of Anita's life.

She didn't feel she was worthy of someone's friendship unless she 'pleased' them. Not only did this make her feel hollow, it seriously affected her self-worth as she grew older.

The Universe has a strange way of teaching us our lessons (remember I said, if you don't deal with a family member who has minimized you, you'll meet that person again and again until you learn how to deal with the situation differently?)

Anita met her Waterloo with a female she had become friends with. Within a very short space of time, she was doing her usual 'people pleasing' stuff and her friend was berating her like a big sister.

The two of them started arguing like sisters and Anita found herself thinking about walking away; that the friendship wasn't worth the stress she was feeling.

But she had an epiphany. She realized the friend wasn't the problem, that she was the problem, and so she decided to use this situation to try doing things differently; to focus on working on her part in the problem and her reactions to the new friend.

By not doing what she had always done, she broke the cycle. She worked on the friendship as an equal partner rather than a little sister trying to please an older sibling.

It didn't happen overnight, but it happened. It was never her new friend's problem, it was always her problem and she was the only one that could fix it.

> 'You can be shattered and then you can put yourself back together piece by piece. What can happen over time is that you wake up one day and realize that you've put yourself back together again completely differently. That you are whole, finally, and strong. But now you are a different shape, a different size.'
>
> —Glennon Doyle Melton

DECIDING TO DO NOTHING

Deciding to do nothing is very different from denying there's a problem.

There will be many occasions when you have tried to get a 'please don't do that' message over to someone, and they just don't get it. I've already said that if you tell someone three times that you're unhappy with something they're doing and they don't hear you, they may never hear you. So rather than beating yourself up and giving yourself stress, if the relationship is important to you, try doing **nothing** for a while.

Meet Rachel

Rachel's husband had massive weight issues which she worried about constantly. Every year she would buy him a new set of gym gear for his birthday (at least one or two sizes bigger than the last set of gym wear she'd bought him) and even bought an expensive gym membership for him. He never wore the clothing and never took up the gym membership.

She came to me for advice as to how she could get him to lose weight. My suggestion was to stop buying gym gear and stop buying gym membership, stop nagging him and stop stressing about him. I urged her to do nothing, say nothing, and to literally get off his case.

Of course, she thought this was a terrible idea, that he was killing himself and she would be left a widow. I asked her whose 'monkey' it was. She firmly believed it was her problem, but it wasn't, it was his. If he chose to eat himself into an early grave, that was his choice and nothing she could ever say or do was going to change his behaviour.

We practised a statement for her to use once he realized she was no longer nagging him.

I asked her to promise me to practice doing nothing.

About six months later he approached her, he was worried that she no longer loved him because she had stopped 'caring' about his weight. She responded with our pre-organised statement:

'Honey, I love you very much, and I do worry about your weight, however, I can't make you do anything you don't want to do, so I have to let you do whatever you want to with regards to your weight.'

It took him another few months, but he came home one day to tell her that he had joined a 'walking group' at the local gym and that every night he was going to walk for an hour with a group of other people with weight issues.

And he did.

Sometimes doing nothing may be your only recourse. Sometimes by you doing nothing, your significant other is forced to do their own something.

> *'Be gentle with your past selves for
> doing what they had to do to get through it.'*
> —Jordan Pickell

WHAT NOT TO DO EVER

Often when we're trying to have our say with someone, our discussion turns into an 'I'm right and you're wrong' argument. We enter a circle that just goes round and round and serves no purpose.

If, when you pluck up the courage to have your say, you feel you've entered this circle, it's OK to step back and say, 'This is getting us nowhere. How about you have a think and I'll have a think and let's see if we can start again. When would be a good time for us to do that?'

WHAT NOT TO SAY EVER

If you've used 'I' statements rather than saying, '**You** are really annoying me when you ....' and if you've stayed calm through your opening statements, the conversation should progress reasonably smoothly.

Avoid starting your conversation with the word 'you', as in, 'You are seriously stressing me when you…'

If your sentences begin with the word 'you', you've already lost the person. Saying 'you' in a conflict situation is tantamount to pointing a finger at them. It's a blame word. Always own the conversation by starting with the word 'I', as in 'I'm having challenges when you …'

Never tell someone to 'calm down'. It's belittling and condescending and will make progressing the conversation so much harder.

Don't use the phrase 'You're not listening to me.' Better to say something like 'I'm not sure if I'm explaining this very well, tell me what you heard me say'.

Remember to watch your 'tone'. If you raise your voice, they will raise theirs and you'll lose the high ground.

Never storm out of the room if things aren't going quite as you'd planned either. Stay the course and keep using the broken record technique.

Above all else, keep breathing.

LIVE TO FIGHT ANOTHER DAY

Sometimes, it's OK not to rush in to deal with a hurtful situation. Sometimes, it's OK to take a step back and look at the bigger picture.

Ask a few questions:

STRATEGIES FOR DEALING WITH BULLYING AT HOME

- Is the situation life-threatening?
- Is the situation urgent?
- Is it just me the person is hurting?
- Am I being too precious?
- Is this just who they are?
- What's the worst that could happen if I leave things a short while?

So, a few tips if you decide not to tackle head-on, the person who is upsetting you.

1. Think through why what they are doing is so hurtful to you. Own it, think through how you can change your reaction rather than attack or walk away.
2. They may have no idea that they're causing you pain. Do they need to know? Rinse and repeat—ask yourself whose monkey it is. If it's yours, own it.
3. You can't change another person, you can only change your reaction to what they are doing or saying
4. You can learn a whole lot about **you** by not reacting the way you've always reacted
5. If you don't learn how to deal with people who upset you, you'll spend a lifetime meeting people who upset you
6. If, after pondering the situation you decide you do need to speak up, then speak up. You are now coming from a place of awareness rather than a place of reaction.
7. Be the bigger person. You have no idea what their background is or what they are going through. Not everything is about you.

'You either get bitter or you get better. It's that simple. You either take what's been dealt to you and allow it to make you a better person, or you allow it to tear you down. The choice doesn't belong to fate, it belongs to you.'

—Josh Shipp

LEARN TO CHOOSE YOUR BATTLES

You've already met my daughter when I shared my experience with the Toughlove group, now I'd like you to meet my son, the child reprobate.

If there was trouble anywhere, he would be in it, near it or causing it. Needless to say, I spent a lot of time and energy berating him.

My daughter in those days, was the good child. Other than leaving her room like a tip, she was a very easy child to care for.

Her comment, 'You treat him better than me. How come he gets away with stuff and I don't?' Great question.

My reply was that if I picked him up on every little thing he did, I would never stop nagging. So, I work on the things he does that I feel are the most important, the most urgent and the behaviours that are more likely to kill him!

My son changed personalities around 11 years of age. He went on to become an amazing sportsman and ultimately a very successful entrepreneur. My daughter earned a Master's degree and became a very successful HR manager, so we all survived.

'Choose your battles wisely. After all, life isn't measured by how many times you stood up to fight. It's not winning battles that makes you happy, but it's how many times you turned away and

chose to look into a better direction. Life is too short to spend it on warring. Fight only the most, most, most important ones, let the rest go.'

—C. JoyBell C.

WHAT TO DO IF *THEIR* BEHAVIOUR SLIPS BACK

It's not unusual when you've had one of these tricky conversations for there to be improvement for a while and then the situation may start slipping back into how things used to be.

The phrase to use then is:

'Remember I asked.......'

'Remember we agreed.......'

we've been there before. circles, we're going in circles, dizzy is all it makes us. We know where it takes us,

There are some people who'll never understand what you're saying or what you're asking. If you've had your conversation several times and nothing has changed, then you may have to accept defeat.

However, in accepting defeat, there are other ways to deal with whatever abuse or poor behaviour you've been experiencing.

If it's a family or close member, you could:

- Not see them so often
- See them only when other people are present

If it's a work colleague, you could lay a formal complaint with a senior manager, that way the behaviour is recorded just in case the person treats others the same way.

If it's a work situation, you could dust off your CV and look for another job. Remember this though, if we don't learn how to deal with inappropriate behaviours in this job, you'll meet someone displaying the same behaviours in your next job. I promise.

If you love your job and it fits in with your family, try to make the relationship work.

> *'If you'd heard me the first time I said it twice,*
> *I wouldn't have had to say it again.'*
> —N'Zuri Za Austin

WHAT TO DO IF *YOU* SLIP BACK INTO OLD HABITS

Here I go again!!

After my marriage broke up and enough time had passed for me to grieve for my lost family, I started dating again. Given that I'd met my husband when I was 18 and was 37 when we split up, I had zero experience of the dating game. I'd met my first husband at a dance, which is how we did it in the 60s so I had no idea how to start or where to start dating in a world where the dating game had changed beyond belief.

I was very clear that I wouldn't get involved with anyone I worked with, it didn't seem wise, so I joined a singles group where I met a man who, on the surface, was a dream come true. He was charming, attentive, seemed quite besotted with me and suddenly he was talking about us moving in together, which to me seemed way too soon. Eventually, he wore me down and he moved into my home with my children.

It was an absolute disaster.

Almost as soon as his suitcases were unpacked, he became a completely different person.

I've often joked that the first time around I married my mother, the second time around I clearly had brought my vile stepfather back into my life. We lasted just three months before I'd had enough of his controlling ways, his anger, his jealousy and his brutal treatment of me and my children. I moved out, even though it was my home. I literally feared for my life.

I got into that terrifying relationship for just over a year and lived with him for less than three months. Every day was a battleground. I had a well-paid job and was able to afford to dress well. I almost had to dress down before I left for work because if I looked too smart it would set him off. If I was late home from work, it would set him off. If I attended a work function, it would set him off.

I knew within a matter of weeks that I needed to get out, but he was living in my house. I alerted my closest friends. They'd witnessed some of his behaviours when they first met him, and if they phoned to see if I was OK, he would say I was out when they knew I wasn't. So they too were getting extremely worried.

Together, my friends and I developed an escape plan just in case I felt the need to get out quickly.

By now, my daughter had moved out and I was pressing a blouse for work one evening when he kicked off.

Out of the blue, he started accusing me of having an affair with someone at work. I had a very hot iron in my hand when he started walking towards me, I was petrified. He tried to grab the iron off me and was bringing it towards my face when I managed to put my arm in front of my face so he couldn't. He did manage to quite badly burn my arm.

I think even he was shocked at what he'd done.

I said 'I'm leaving. Don't try to stop me.' I called my son and told him to get in the car. We literally walked out with what we were standing up in.

I went to my friend's home as we had pre-planned and they insisted we call the police. When the police arrived and saw the burns on my arm, they asked me a question which utterly freaked me out. They asked, 'Does he have a gun in the house?' I said he had. Ostensibly he went rabbit shooting, but a gun is a gun.

The police immediately went to the house to question him. He put on his shocked and stunned act telling the police that I was delusional—that he'd done nothing wrong, that I was the problem, but they'd seen the burns on my arm. They warned him to stay away from me and that they were requesting an immediate restraining order to keep me safe.

After the police left him, they came back to ask what I wanted to do about the situation. I said I want to leave, but he's in my house and all my things are there. I need to be able to get back into the house tomorrow to pack some immediate things for myself and my son and I need him not to be there. Then I want to organize a removal truck for Saturday to pack up my furniture and put it into storage while I look for rental accommodation. The police were amazing. I'm assuming they then went back to him to tell him to keep out of my way the next day; that the restraining order would be in place within 24 hours and that I would be moving out on the following Saturday.

On the day of the move, my friends brought several burly men with them so we knew he wouldn't cause any trouble. Bullies are cowards.

I never went back.

He started frantically calling me at work with his usual message. 'I'm so sorry, it's just that I love you so much, I'm terrified of losing you.' By treating me the way he did, he guaranteed that's exactly what happened.

How the heck did I get into such a mess again and so quickly?

A lovely friend once told me that where relationships were concerned, she 'got in too fast, and out too slow', which summed up what had just happened to me.

I beat myself up for months for being so stupid, but eventually I had to accept that I had to treat the terrifying episode as yet another learning opportunity. I had to credit myself that as soon as I realised I was in a dangerous situation and that I'd put my kids into a dangerous situation, I got us out of there.

I said earlier, never tackle a bully, and I 100% mean that. You hear of women leaving and then being persuaded to return, numerous times. Each time they leave and go back, the bully gets worse because the person has dared to stand up to them: they have dared to leave.

If, as you read this, you feel you've made that same mistake, possibly several times, don't beat yourself up. Learn from the experience, applaud yourself for escaping.

Some women never escape from such men.

Some women die at their hands.

> 'In a healthy relationship, vulnerability is wonderful. It leads to increased intimacy and closer bonds. When a healthy person realizes that he or she hurt you, they feel remorse and they make amends. It's safe to be honest. In an abusive system, vulnerability is dangerous. It's considered a weakness, which acts as an invitation for more mistreatment. Abusive people feel a surge of power when they discover a weakness. They exploit it, using it to gain more power. Crying or complaining confirms that they've poked you in the right spot.'
>
> —Christina Enevoldsen, *The Rescued Soul: The Writing Journey for the Healing of Incest and Family Betrayal*

CHAPTER 6
YOUR FUTURE IS COMING READY OR NOT

> *The journey begins with a teacher,*
> *someone who pulls you and pushes you*
> *with a big stick called 'truth'*
>
> —Goethe

LEARNING TO FORGIVE

Forgiving my ex-husband took a while; forgiving my mother for her neglect took a bit longer but forgiving my stepfather for the abuse I suffered at his hands took years.

When I first started having counselling the subject of forgiveness came up and my reaction was 'I will never forgive him' to which the counsellor replied 'Then you will carry this burden to your grave and it could possibly put you into an early grave'.

Which hit home. I'd had all manner of health issues in my later life, down to carrying the baggage I'm sure. Even after he died, I was still carrying the hurt.

So I worked on forgiving him for my sake not for his. Forgiving him didn't mean I could forget what happened, but I realised that by having so much counselling, it had led me to becoming a counsellor. I wouldn't have done that if he hadn't been in my life.

Ultimately, I realised that holding on to the pain and the trauma would probably wreck my life. It was in the past, it was over, I couldn't change what had happened. I really did have to 'let go and let God'. So I did.

Did my forgiveness come overnight with a bolt of lightning? Absolutely not. I acknowledge it took me many years. I was so determined that he wasn't going to wreck the rest of my life I was prepared to do anything to get him out of my head.

> 'Forgiveness is above all a personal choice, a decision of the heart to go against our natural instinct to pay back evil with evil.'
> —Pope John Paul II

WHAT IF YOU 'CHOSE' YOUR PARENTS?

I was attending another weird workshop, mostly around building my self-esteem and getting on with my life when attendees were asked another strange question:

'What if you chose your parents?'

That question really did blow my mind. My reaction: 'You must be joking, why would I choose a mother who is never home and a stepfather who abuses me?'

The facilitator simply said, 'I'll leave that thought with you'.

What that question does, once you recover from the shock and the rage at the thought you'd choose two awful people to be your parents, is that it forces you to consider their qualities.

My mother became an amazing geriatric nurse in her later years. She was a brilliant knitter; she could turn out stunning sweaters, cardigans, even knitted dresses. She was a stunning embroiderer. I still have some of the tablecloths she embroidered, and she was a fabulous singer, great cook and passionate gardener.

My stepfather was a brilliant mathematician; he qualified for university at 14. He was a classical violinist; he could play just about any musical instrument and actually did complex crosswords in ink. He was an organic gardener long before it became fashionable.

I was able, in the end, to rebuild my relationship with my mother, but no matter his qualities, I chose not to rebuild my relationship with my stepfather.

However, the question did at least let me acknowledge his talents.

> 'Nobody is all good or bad and nobody all light or dark. Every human being has so many different aspects and facets to them. There can be something noble and something really dark and dangerous going on in a person all at the same time.'
>
> —Anna Gunn

LEARNING TO SAY NO SO YOU HAVE THE TIME AND ENERGY TO SAY YES

It takes immense courage to start standing up for yourself, to start saying 'That's not OK' or 'I will no longer accept that treatment'.

Only the unhealthy or unhappy people in your life, whether that's at work or in your private life, will abuse you. Yes, we may have an argument with someone, but if the other person has a healthy self-esteem, that's as far as the argument should go. They won't turn the situation into a vendetta or a revenge mission.

Be gentle with yourself always. You may take some steps forward and then slip back. That's OK. It's normal. Just be 100% determined that your slipping back is just a lapse, it isn't a retreat into your old ways.

Meet Jackie

Jackie is a lovely woman. Gentle, kind, loyal, a hard worker. She had left an abusive marriage when her children were barely out of nappies. She worked hard at whatever jobs she could get and which fit in with her children's daycare and then school hours.

She kept meeting bullies. Her personality (Dove) made her a sitting duck to everyone and anyone who had a grudge to bear against society.

She would change jobs. She changed jobs numerous times. By now she was early 50s and it's way harder to find new jobs at 50 than when you're in your 30s.

She changed jobs yet again and met yet another awful man. She couldn't work out whether he was a bully, a harasser, a narcissist or a combination of all three awful personality traits.

She confessed he was the worst person she'd ever met, even after a lifetime of meeting bullies.

From day one, he seemed to have her in his sights. She watched him very carefully and did everything she could to keep out of his way. He seemed to have a 'women' issue because while she worked for him, she saw an endless stream of bright, intelligent women leave because of his treatment of them.

Finally, despite having no job to go to, she left. Her health was in dire straits and she knew if she didn't leave she was going to get seriously ill.

After a period of healing and grieving time with no income, she got mad. She got so mad that she decided to lay a case against him. She had a female lawyer friend who offered to represent her for free and they took him on.

It was a singularly unpleasant experience. It took a massive toll on her health, but she was 100% determined on two counts:

- That no one was ever going to bully her again. Ever.
- To mark this man's card for the treatment of all the women he kept abusing

Her settlement was meagre in the scheme of things, but she fought him, called him out and won her case.

> 'The quiet but inexorable breaking down of self-esteem is much more sinister – it's violation of the soul.'
> —Rachel Abbott, *Only the Innocent*

BECOME YOUR OWN BEST FRIEND

Learning to love ourselves is such a tumultuous journey. I have no idea why we beat ourselves up so regularly and so viciously, but there will come a time in your life where you will realise you're a pretty special person.

Yes, you've made mistakes, sometimes the same ones several times over, but you're still here, you're still functioning and you are absolutely special.

Start to be kind to yourself. It doesn't mean you'll never make a mistake again, of course you will. The difference now, I hope, is that you'll own your own behaviours; be responsible for the decisions you make; be aware of the people you want to keep in your life and the ones you've decided it's OK to let go of.

Sometimes, life really is one step forward and one, two or even three steps backwards. The main thing is to get up each day and start the rest of your life utterly believing in yourself.

It's OK to give yourself a good talking to now and again. It's OK to acknowledge you've just made another mistake. It's OK to say I've just learned another important lesson from that mistake. It's OK to say 'I am an amazing person and I love being me'.

Start listening to yourself. You really are the smartest person in your life.

> *'It's perfectly OK to talk to yourself and it's perfectly OK to answer yourself. But it's totally sad that you have to repeat what you said because you weren't listening.'*
>
> —Ifunny.co

CHAPTER 7
YOU'RE NEVER TOO OLD AND IT'S NEVER TOO LATE

> 'Here's a test to find out if your mission on earth is finished: If you are alive, it isn't.'
>
> —Richard Bach

SETTING UP A FUTURE WHERE NAYSAYERS, ABUSERS AND BULLIES KEEP OUT OF YOUR WAY BECAUSE THEY KNOW YOU NO LONGER PLAY THAT GAME

I talked to my black belt granddaughter about how she now copes with bullies and her response was that they mostly don't come near her now.

Her training in Taekwondo changed her self-belief and her energy. It's almost as if she can now give people a certain 'look' and they move on.

KEEPING YOUR SELF-ESTEEM INTACT NOW AND FOREVER

If you've been through the mill again, don't give up.

The journey to feeling good about yourself isn't a one-off, it doesn't happen and stay that way for the rest of your life, you have to keep working on it.

Some tips for maintaining a healthy self-esteem:

- Fake it till you make it
- Be proud of the gifts you've been given and use them
- Surround yourself with positive people
- Join something that interests you
- Give back—become a volunteer
- Try new things
- Keep being assertive
- Set some goals
- Work out the God-given talents you've been gifted and use them

> *'If they don't like you for being yourself,
> be yourself even more.'*
> —Taylor Swift

WHAT'S YOUR WHAT NEXT?

Now you've dealt with the people and situations in your life that were dragging you down, what now, what next?

Have you set some goals for your next step?

Have you created a whole new career path for yourself?

I had a recent conversation with a female lawyer, and I saw from her card that she had been a teacher. I asked what made her leave teaching to take up the law. She said she was tired of being endlessly undervalued by the education system and by so many parents, so she decided she was worth more than that and took up law.

Which I found interesting because the legal profession isn't known for its amazing treatment of female lawyers.

She acknowledged that her first job as a lawyer was as bad if not worse than her teaching experience. She was the only female in a law firm of around 100 male lawyers and it was 'assumed' that she would want to take over their family law portfolio.

She didn't.

She stuck around for a while to get a decent amount of time on her CV and then started researching law firms with at least 50% female lawyers and applied and was accepted into that law firm.

> 'She believed she could, so she did.'
> —R S Gray

WHERE WOULD YOU AIM IF YOU KNEW YOU COULDN'T FAIL?

Take a few minutes to answer the following questions.

1. What would you like more of in your life?
2. What would you like 'less' of in your life?
3. What has been your greatest achievement to date?
4. Have you forgiven yourself for mistakes you made?
5. What has been the biggest lesson in your life?
6. Who is your greatest supporter?

7. Who is your biggest detractor?
8. If money was no object, what you would do differently?
9. If you were younger/better qualified/smarter, what would you do differently?
10. If you won Lotto what would you do differently?

AS ONE DOOR CLOSES, ANOTHER ALWAYS OPENS

During Covid, my business closed down literally overnight. My conference bookings were cancelled and the teams I'd been working with had all been sent home during lockdown.

I used that time to write a book *Women Behaving Courageously* as a result of a neighbour telling me how the bank she worked for had decided to reduce staff numbers as a result of the pandemic.

They asked all the women to reapply for their jobs with the intention of culling numbers, but all the men got to keep their jobs, no questions asked.

She was furious.

At the book launch, so many women asked if I planned to run workshops based on the book. I hadn't planned to but because of the response, decided it was time to resurrect them.

I went back through all my old notes to prepare my second entré into running women's workshops.

One of the women's workshops I run every now and again is called, 'I know I'm here to do something amazing if I could only work out what that is.' And it fills rooms.

So many of us 'settle' for something safe; something comfortable; something that isn't too stressful. Most of the career counselling I do with people seems to be with men in their 40s and women in their 50s or even 60s. They often ask for help with stress or sleepless nights, or even depression which always leads to a conversation about their childhood and their early aspirations.

Invariably they'll tell me that their parents urged them into a 'safe' career and so people who dreamed of becoming musicians, or artists, found themselves in jobs that literally bored them into all manner of health issues.

We begin by working on a series of questions:

- What did you want to 'be' when you were younger?
- Why did you let that dream go?
- Is it something you could pick up again?
- What would that take?
- Could it simply become a hobby?
- Could you turn it into a passive income?
- Could the challenge you're currently dealing with actually be your life's purpose?

Meet Cathy

I met Cathy when I was working with a group of theatre nurses. They were all exhausted and this was a team day put on by the hospital as respite for them and a thank you for always being amazing no matter the crisis.

I always talk to people about their 'What next?'

It was something someone asked me after I'd literally just been promoted and picked up my first company car. It stopped me in my tracks. I was delighted with my promotion and had zero thoughts at that stage about any what next. The person who asked me suggested we should always have our next step planned and be prepared for it.

Cathy had been talking about her fear of the future. She was nearing 60 and was finding working as a theatre nurse more difficult with each passing year. So I posed the 'what next' question.

She had no idea. So I asked what her hobbies were and she told me she adored growing and selling herbs at the local farmers market. I wondered if working with herbs full-time was an option. She explained that she and her husband still had a mortgage and she simply couldn't afford to give up her salary.

We brainstormed a few ideas. Could she:

- Put aside 10% of her salary for the next six months to create a business start-up fund? Yes, she could.
- Could she then work just four days a week in surgery and work three days a week with herbs? Yes, she could.
- Could she set a goal to then work three days a week and four days a week with her herbs? Yes, she could.

Within 18 months Cathy was working just one or two days a week in her nursing job and the rest of her week was now spent in her lucrative herb business. She planned to retire full-time from nursing within the next 12 months.

Q: What's your what next?

Q: What would you do differently if money wasn't an issue?

Q: Could you, in two to three years, change your entire career path the way Cathy did?

'Our goals can only be reached through a vehicle of a plan, in which we must fervently believe, and upon which we must vigorously act. There is no other route to success.'

—Pablo Picasso

CHAPTER 8
FEEL THE FEAR AND MOVE AHEAD ANYWAY

> 'The definition of insanity is to keep doing what you've always done while expecting a different outcome.'
>
> —Albert Einstein

THE JOURNEY OF 1000 MILES STARTS WITH A SINGLE STEP

Changing our lives so we're not used and abused takes time. Close family will be shocked that their placid family member doesn't seem to be so placid any longer, in fact, he/she has become rather stroppy.

You may lose friends because you're no longer a people pleaser and you refuse to loan them money to people any longer. If that's the case, they weren't really friends in the first place.

Your work colleagues may give you a wide berth for a while until they realise that you're still you but a stronger you, a more assertive you.

Some of your family, friends and co-workers may want to know how you got to be so strong and may even ask if you can teach them how to be more assertive.

Now the real journey begins. You will need to find ways to stay strong, to not be lured back into the target you used to be.

DO REGULAR MENTAL/PHYSICAL/SPIRITUAL CHECKS

When you first start standing up for yourself, you'll experience a massive high. You did it. You stood up to whoever was trying to bring you down and you're still standing. Well done.

Then ordinary life takes over and the exhilaration wears off. Books will fall off shelves for you; people will appear in your life with the exact message you need to hear right now. Maybe you have another encounter with someone where you don't say the right things and you come away feeling pathetic and annoyed with yourself. AGAIN.

Assertiveness is a bit like physical fitness. You don't go to the gym once and expect the results to last forever. You have to keep working at your fitness, and so it is with working on yourself—your self-esteem and self-worth.

There are so many ways you can keep working on you:

- Join a gym
- Join a group of like minded people
- Surround yourself with positive people
- Decide to either let go of the people who drag you down or if it's a family member simply spend less time with them
- Invest in a journal—write in it every day
- Start your day with something positive and end your day with something thoughtful

- Start planning your 5-year goals
- Join a night class and learn something fun, joyful and outrageous

The critical thing is, don't slip back into your old friendships, old behaviours and old patterns.

> *'If you realized how powerful your thoughts are, you'd never think a negative thought again.'*
> —Peace Pilgrim

BELIEVE IN MIRACLES

I absolutely and totally believe in miracles. I've had so many amazing things happen to me that I can only put them down to someone somewhere looking after me.

Books will literally fall off shelves for you; people will appear in your life with the exact message you need to hear right now.

The right people have always appeared for me when I've been down or struggling with my latest dumb move. This book on bullying was never on my radar until my friend of over 20 years said she'd received a message for me.

Janice is a channeler, and it's fascinating to sit with her. The two of us can be having a perfectly normal conversation when I'll notice she tips her head to one side. I now know that's her body language when a 'message' is coming through. In the early days of knowing her, it was quite freaky, now I love the messages she gives me. It's so affirming to know that we do have helpers if we are just willing to be open to the messages.

Trust the process. Be kind to yourself.

'The biggest lesson I've learned is: It's OK for me to be kind to myself. It's OK to be wrong. It's OK to get mad. It's OK to be flawed. It's OK to be happy. It's OK to move on.'

—Hayley Williams

KNOW YOU'RE SUPPORTED

I also know that if I'm having a bad day, someone will phone me to say, 'I was just thinking about you and hoping you're OK?' It's absolutely amazing how that works.

My grandmother has been dead for over 50 years, but I still talk to her. I simply imagine she is with me all the time. If I'm having a problem, I ask her thoughts on the solution, and then I wait. I can guarantee that within the hour the answer will pop into my head. Is that my gran sending me messages? I have no idea, all I know is that having her with me is a massive comfort, and when I ask a question and get an answer, I feel totally supported.

Give it a go.

YOU'VE JUST CLIMBED YOUR MOUNTAIN

If you're still with me; if you've done the exercises in the book; if you've taken that first step to say to someone, 'I will not be treated this way', you really have moved your mountain.

Imagine if, when you were born, on a subconscious level you've always known what you are here for; what you are here to do.

The amazing thing about being abused or treated badly, which on the surface seems to be so unfair, is that once you have dealt with your abuse, you will teach someone else how to deal with theirs.

You will become an 'influencer'.

Or better still, what if the trauma you've just overcome is actually your life's purpose? What if you had to overcome that trauma to teach others how to overcome theirs?

Wherever you go with your beautiful new energy, people will gravitate towards you, some will want to help you grow even farther and some will want to know how you became so amazing.

Keep being you.

> 'There is a vitality, a life force, a quickening that is translated through you into action, and because there is only one of you in all time, this expression is unique. And if you block it, it will never exist through any other medium and will be lost.'
>
> —Martha Graham

CHAPTER 9
FURTHER RESOURCES

GREAT QUOTES IF YOU EVER FEEL YOU ARE SLIPPING BACK INTO OLD VICTIM BEHAVIOURS

'When someone shows you who they are, believe them the first time.'

—Maya Angelou

'If you're horrible to me, I'm going to write a song about it, and you won't like it. That's how I operate.'

—Taylor Swift

'The quiet but inexorable breaking down of self-esteem is much more sinister - it's violation of the soul.'

—Rachel Abbott

'It's not the words or the actions you should trust, rather the pattern.'

—Shannon L. Alder

*'So the girl watched her brothers grow and play and sing their songs and go to University. She kept quiet and good and waited for the blessings of

God to bring her joy and peace. They did not come, the blessings. Nor did the joy or the peace. Instead she was disturbed at all times by frustration and rage that burst out of her at inappropriate moments.'

—Meg Bignell, *The Angry Woman's Choir*

'I believe that many modern women, my mother included, carry within them a whole secret New England cemetery, wherein they have quietly buried—in neat little rows—the personal dreams they have given up for their families.'

—Elizabeth Gilbert

'When a toxic person can no longer control you, they will try to control how others see you. The misinformation will seem unfair but rise above it, trusting that others will eventually see the truth, just as you did.'

—Jill Blakeway, healer and author

'Scar tissue is stronger than regular tissue. Realize its strength.'

—Henry Rollins, American musician

'Pain travels through families until someone is ready to feel it.'

—Stephi Wagner

'Sometimes you have to make a decision that will break your heart but give peace to your soul.'

—Unknown

'Don't wait until everything is just right. It will never be perfect. There will always be challenges, obstacles, and less-than-perfect conditions. So what? Get started now. With each step you take, you will grow stronger and stronger, more and more skilled, more and more self-confident, and more and more successful.'

—Mark Victor Hansen

FURTHER RESOURCES

'Vengeance is the act of turning anger in on yourself. On the surface it may be directed at someone else, but it's a sure-fire recipe for arresting emotional recovery.'

—Jane Goldman

'As women, we must speak out, speak up, say no to our inheritance of loss and yes to a future of women-led dialogue about women's rights and value.'

—Zainab Salbi

'I've been absolutely terrified every moment of my life—and I've never let it keep me from doing a single thing I wanted to do.'

—Georgia O'Keefe

'The most courageous act is still to think for yourself. Aloud.'

—Coco Chanel

'When they discover the centre of the universe, a lot of people will be disappointed to discover they are not it.'

—Bernard Bailey

'Beginning today, treat everyone you meet as if they were going to be dead by midnight. Extend to them all the care, kindness and understanding you can muster, and do it with no thought of any reward. Your life will never be the same again.'

—Og Mandino

'Being a woman is a terribly difficult task since it consists primarily in dealing with men.'

—Joseph Conrad

'I'm slowly learning that some people are not good for me, no matter how much I love them.'

—Michelle K

'Everyone, I say, stop bullying, it's sad and tears someone's heart apart and next thing they do is Suicide because they think that is the right next step! If you're a person who gets bullied find someone who will stop this! Don't just kill yourself for the other person to be happy because you're gone! They're just jealous of you and want to start problems and make you a troublemaker. Because bullying is a dumb and stupid waste of time!'

—Skye Daphne

'...here's what I've learned—people will hurt you, but you don't have to respond—not every mean comment or cruel act deserves to be noticed...'

—John Geddes

'What a desperate, pathetic fool I was. Time after time, my "friends" had shown me their true colors. Yet, I still wanted to believe they were sorry for causing me pain.'

—Jodee Blanco

'Remember it's your job to stick up for yourself. Don't wait for the cavalry. You ARE the cavalry.'

—Matthew Hussey

'We repeat what we don't repair.'

—Dr Sharon Martin

'Life is a fight, but not everyone's a fighter. Otherwise, bullies would be an endangered species.'

—Andrew Vachss

'Even in your rightness about a subject, when you try to push your rightness toward another who disagrees, no matter how right you are, it *causes more pushing against. In other words, it isn't until you stop pushing that any real allowing of what you want can take place.'*

—Esther (and Abraham and Jerry)

'The scars from mental cruelty can be as deep and long-lasting as wounds from punches or slaps but are often not as obvious. Even among women who have experienced violence from a partner, half or more report that the man's emotional abuse is what is causing them the greatest harm.'

—Lundy Bancroft

'Don't run back to old ways just because they're more comfortable or easier to access. Remember you left certain habits and people for a reason: to better your life. You can't move forward with your life if you keep going back.'

—Vex King

'Live life as if everything is rigged in your favour.'

—Rumi

'When someone isn't treating you right, no matter how much you love them, you've got to love yourself more and walk away.'

—Helen Majeshi

'The problem is women think he'll change. He won't. Men make the mistake of thinking she will never leave. She will.'

—The MindsJournal.com

MY 40-YEAR READING LIST (ALPHABETICAL)

I'm hopeful that all these books are still in print, but if not, check the titles. The titles alone will be of comfort.

Women's books

'Adult children of divorce'. Dr Edward W Beal & Gloria Hochman

'Breaking free of the Co-dependency trap'. Barry K. Weinhold, Ph.D and Jane B. Weinhold, Ph.D

'Co-dependence. Misunderstood – Mistreated'. Anne Wilson Schael

'Children of Chaos'. Douglas Rushkoff

'Coping with difficult people'. Robert M. Bramson, Ph.D

'Dealing with the tough stuff'. How to achieve results from crucial conversations. Darren Hill, Alison Hill & Dr Sean Richardson

'Desert Flower'. Waris Dirie and Cathleen Miller

Don't say 'YES' when you want to say 'NO'. Herbert Fensterheim Ph.D and Jeanm Baer

'Dutiful Daughters'. Edited by Jean McCrindle and Shiela Rowbotham

'Emotional Blackmail'. When the people in your life use fear, obligation and guilt to manipulate you. Dr Susan Forward with Donna Frazier

'Feel the fear and do it anyway'. Susan Jeffers

'Games people play'. The psychology of human relationships. Eric Berne, MD

'Her mother's daughter'. Marilyn French

'How come every time I get stabbed in the back my fingerprints are on the knife? And other meditation on MANAGEMENT'. Jerry B. Harvey

'I am right you are wrong'. From this to the New Renaissance: from Rock Logic to Water Logic. Edward de Bono

'I'm OK – You're OK'. Thomas A. Harris, MD

'I'm OK. You're not so hot'. Dolph Sharp

'Man's Search for Meaning'. Viktor E Frankle

'Mothers and Daughters'. Evan Hunter

'Not without my daughter'. Betty Mahmoody

'Resolving conflicts. How to turn conflict into co-operation'. Wendy Grant

'Staying OK.' Amy Bjork Harris and Thomas A. Harris MD

'The couple who became each other'. David L. Calof with Robin Simons

'The dance of anger'. Harriet G. Lerner

'The dance of deception'. Harriet G. Lerner

'The dance of Intimacy'. Harriett G. Lerner

'The disease to please'. Harriet B. Braiker, Ph.D

'The dance of the dissident daughter'. A woman's journey from Christian Tradition to the Sacred Feminine. Sue Monk Kidd

'The eight essential steps to conflict resolution'. Preserving relationships at work, at home and in the community. Dudly Weeks, Ph.D

'The handmaiden's tale'. Margaret Attwood

'The life you were born to live'. Dan Millman

'The perfection trap'. Thomas Curran

'The way of the peaceful warrior'. Dan Millman

'When I say no, I feel guilty'. Manuel J Smith, Ph.D

'Women who love too much'. Robin Norwood

Dysfunctional workplaces

'Bad leadership'. Barbara Kellerman

'The addictive organization'. Anne Wilso Schaef

'The enemy within'. Richard W. Buchanan

'The FIVE dysfunctions of a team'. Patrick Lencioni

'The no Asshole rule'. Building a civilized workplace and surviving one that isn't. Robert I. Sutton. Ph.D

'Why teams don't work'. Harvey Robbins & Michale Finley

'Workplace Bullying. The costly business secret'. Andrea W. Needham

Books of hope

'Feel the fear and do it anyway'. Susan Jeffers

'I want to change but I don't know how'. Tom Rusk & Randy Read

'Man's Search for Meaning'. Viktor E Frankle

'Success is never ending, failure is never final'. Robert H. Schuller

'The angry woman's choir'. Fiction. Meg Bignell

'The hungry spirit'. Charles Handy

'The search for meaning'. Charles Handy

'The Purpose of your life'. Carol Adrienne

'Tough times never last, but tough people do!'. Robert H. Schuller

'UNBOUND. A Woman's Guide to Power'. Kasia Urbaniak

'You can heal your life'. Louise Hay

Further reading

'The bully, the bullied and the bystander'. Barbara Coloroso

'Queen Bees and Wannabes for the Facebook Generation: Helping your teenage daughter survive cliques, gossip, bullying and boyfriends'. Rosalind Wiseman

RESOURCES IF YOUR CHILD IS BEING BULLIED

'No, It's Not Ok: How to stop the cycle of bullying'. Tania Roxborough and Kim Stephenson

'Bullying is a pain in the brain'. Trevor Romain

'How to handle bullying: A kid's guide on how to spot and how to stop bullying'. Samuel John

Empoweringparents.com. How to deal with child rage

COUNSELLING SERVICES IN NEW ZEALAND

Youthline – 0800 376 633

Lifeline – 0800 543 354

AA (The alcohol and drug helpline) – 0800 787 797

Al-Anon Family Groups – 0508 425 266

NZ Mental Health Services

Samaritans – 0800 726 666

Suicide Crisis Helpline – 0508 828 865

Healthline – 0800 611 116

Toughlove Groups – 09 624 4363

ABOUT THE AUTHOR

I had no plans to write this book. I was a long way through writing *'I know I'm here to do something amazing if I could only work out what that is'*, a book for people who were in a career or life crisis, but sometimes the Universe has different plans for us.

Didn't someone once say, we make plans, God laughs?

I was pottering along working with a couple of teams, preparing for two conferences and writing the new book when I had a terrifying health incident. I couldn't breathe, I felt as though I was in labour and I started vomiting. The incident lasted several hours and literally scared the life out of me. Then the incident was over and I had no idea what had triggered it.

The very next day, I received a call from a friend of mine who 'channels' she said 'I have a message for you. An urgent message.

I've been told to tell you that you need to put the book you're writing aside and write one on bullying'.

I was stunned, amazed and not a little bit perplexed because working on bullying hadn't been a major part of my career. Conflict yes; toxic teams for sure; terrible managers absolutely but bullying not so much.

In fact, my immediate reaction was 'NO, please don't ask me to do that. I'm over all that stuff I dealt with; I've moved on; I don't want to revisit any part of what happened to me when I was younger.'

However, when you get a 'call' or a literal whack on the side of the head as I'd had with my health scare, I believe you're duty-bound to answer it.

Once I started thinking about writing the book, I realized bullying had been the central theme of my life once I went to live with my mother and stepfather. I endured 12 years of it. So perhaps helping others tackle bullies was *my* destiny!

Once my marriage ended and I set off on the course of working in HR, another thing I'd never planned, I started meeting amazing people. People who led me and encouraged me and opened doors for me. Doors that led me into this particular career direction.

I've truly felt guided and I've truly been blessed.

Perhaps it really wasn't a coincidence that I was asked to tackle bullying when I remembered that the quote I have on the cover of my women's workbook is:

> 'You've been assigned this mountain so you can show others it can be moved'.
> —Mel Robbins

BOOKS BY THE AUTHOR

Shift Your But (Self-published 1999)

Finding the Square Root of a Banana (Self-published 2000)

Did I Really Employ You? (Reed Publishing (NZ), 2004)

Excellent Employment: Hiring the best people to help your business grow (Published by A & C Black, UK, 2007)

Mum's the Word by Vanessa Sunde, Kenina Court and Ann Andrews (Published by Phantom Publishing, 2007)

Lessons in Leadership: 50 Ways to Avoid Falling into the 'Trump' Trap (Published by Moreau Publishing, 2017)

Leaders Behaving Badly: What happens when ordinary people show up, stand up and speak up (Activity Press, 2018)

My Dear Franchisees, 2nd Edition (Activity Press, 2019). First published 2006.

Women Behaving Courageously: How gutsy women, young and old are transforming the world' (Activity Press, 2020).

Women Behaving Courageously: The Workbook (Activity Press, 2022)

For more information and to stay up to date with new releases, visit: https://annandrews.co.nz

ACKNOWLEDGMENTS

My first thanks will always go to my beloved grandparents. They really were my guiding lights.

A massive thanks to the women at the Citizens Advice Bureau, Glenfield, who persuaded me to train as a counsellor. It was while I was training to be a marriage guidance counsellor with the CAB that my marriage collapsed. I've often joked that I'm not sure whether I came bottom of that training course or top. I believe I came top because it helped me realise that the marriage I was in was hollow and the course gave me the courage to walk away.

Once I was back in the workplace, I started meeting people who saw things in me that I'd stopped seeing myself.

David for giving me my first job as a personnel assistant and then recommending me for my first role as a personnel manager in my own right. Michael, my general manager, who gave me the opportunity to experiment with self-managing teams. Coral my co-personnel manager for always being there for me when both of us were being bullied by a female manager. Anthony for saving my sanity when I realized I'd moved from the frying pan to the fire when I became HR manager of a tech company and who let me loose on his team in Wellington.

Thanks to all the brave owners, managers and franchisors who have trusted me to work with their teams or asked me to speak at their conferences.

Thanks to Covid. Without the pandemic I would never have heard Hannah's story and decided to write my *Women Behaving Courageously* book. Thanks to all the women who bravely attended my women's workshops where they absolutely felt the fear and did it anyway.

Thanks to Orquidea who trusted me to work with her beautiful diversional therapists: to AJ who became my tech man running things behind the scenes for my webinars.

To Mary and David who were determined to set up a self-managed team in their franchise even though I'd given up on self-managed teams some years before, not because they didn't work, but because they worked too well.

Thanks also go to longtime friends Clare, Pam and newly found friends Annette and Linda. Four women who have encouraged me every step of the way with this new and unexpected book.

To Janice for passing on the message that rocked my complacency and made me do what it seems I was here to do.

To Martin Taylor my amazing publisher, who takes my rantings and knocks them into a shape that makes sense.

My final thanks as always go to my husband and partner of 30 years, Warren (an Owl) who is always there for me and never loses patience when mid-sentence I head into my office with another idea for something I need to add to the book.

My experience is that people come into our lives for a reason, a season or for life. Bless the people who are in your life for life.

SOURCES

CHAPTER 1

https://www.psychologytoday.com/nz/blog/your-emotional-meter/202404/family-relationship-patterns

https://www.nhs.uk/mental-health/self-help/tips-and-support/raise-low-self-esteem/

https://www.psychologytoday.com/nz/blog/childhood-emotional-neglect/202403/the-well-meaning-parent-who-grew-up-emotionally-neglected

Las Vegas sixth grader, 12, commits suicide after school bullying (nypost.com)

https://mentalhealth.org.nz/suicide-prevention/statistics-on-suicide-in-new-zealand

https://www.unicef.org.nz/media-releases/new-report-card-shows-that-new-zealand-is-failing-its-children

https://parentingteensandtweens.com/forty-of-the-most-inspiring-heartfelt-quotes-about-raising-teens/#:~:text=Don't%20sacrifice%20your%20teen's,for%20a%20more%20peaceful%20today.%E2%80%9D

CHAPTER 2

Why Can't People Be More Like Me?: Using simple psychology to understand yourself and others: Edwards, Andy: 9781838137908: Amazon.com: Books

https://www.choosingtherapy.com/self-worth-vs-self-esteem/#:~:text=Self%2Desteem%20describes%20how%20you,or%20the%20approval%20of%20others.&text=Self%2Dworth%20is%20a%20more,your%20worth%20as%20a%20person.

www.anxietycentre.com/tests/self-esteem-

CHAPTER 3

https://www.forbes.com/sites/carolinecastrillon/2023/06/04/10-signs-its-time-to-leave-a-toxic-workplace/?sh=4938223506c2

CHAPTER 4

https://www.betterhelp.com/advice/bullying/are-you-being-bullied-5-examples-of-bullying/
https://compassionit.com/2016/02/11/what-is-bullying-and-what-isnt-bullying/
https://www.verywellmind.com/how-to-confront-workplace-bullying-460682
https://www.verywellmind.com/why-do-people-bully-5187244
https://www.pacer.org/bullying/info/questions-answered/bullying-harassment.asp
https://www.gsb.stanford.edu/insights/how-narcissistic-leaders-destroy-within
https://www.psychologytoday.com/nz/blog/bully-wise/202007/the-bully-narcissist-work-toolbox-coping
https://institute.crisisprevention.com/Refresh-AU-De-Escalation-Tips.html/
https://theconversation.com/are-you-a-bully-without-even-knowing-it-heres-how-to-tell-105874
10 Good Reasons to Shut the Hell Up - The Good Men Project
https://www.drcraigmalkin.com/#about
https://www.psychologytoday.com/nz/basics/sociopathy
https://www.psychologytoday.com/nz/basics/narcissism#the-traits-of-narcissism
https://www.psychologytoday.com/nz/blog/bully-wise/202007/the-bully-narcissist-work-toolbox-coping
https://www.researchgate.net/publication/247720311_Adaptation_to_Self-Managing_Work_Teams
https://hbr.org/2004/01/narcissistic-leaders-the-incredible-pros-the-inevitable-cons
https://www.researchgate.net/publication/318641581_Narcissism_in_Leadership_and_Management_A_Research_Summary
https://www.psychologytoday.com/nz/blog/compassion-matters/201211/is-social-media-blame-the-rise-in-narcissism
https://www.psychologytoday.com/nz/blog/communication-success/201711/5-traits-of-positive-narcissism-and-their-downfalls
https://iohrm.appstate.edu/faculty/dr-shawn-bergman

CHAPTER 5

https://www.marriage.com/advice/relationship/relationship-bullying/
https://www.healthyplace.com/blogs/verbalabuseinrelationships/2022/4/do-i-attract-abusive-relationships
https://www.nhs.uk/mental-health/talking-therapies-medicine-treatments/

talking-therapies-and-counselling/cognitive-behavioural-therapy-cbt/
overview/
https://www.thehealthy.com/family/relationships/abusive-relationship-quotes/
https://hbr.org/2015/11/how-to-make-sure-youre-heard-in-a-difficult-
conversation
https://www.pacer.org/bullying/info/stats.asp
https://www.psychologytoday.com/nz/blog/communication-success/201504/10-
signs-your-co-worker-or-colleague-is-a-narcissist
https://www.linkedin.com/in/stephen-m-johnson-ph-d-79098315/
https://www.psychologytoday.com/nz/blog/the-human-beast/202402/why-
narcissism-is-rising
https://www.mayoclinic.org/diseases-conditions/narcissistic-personality-
disorder/symptoms-causes/syc-20366662
https://www.mayoclinic.org/healthy-lifestyle/childrens-health/in-depth/mental-
illness-in-children/art-20046577

CHAPTER 9

Creating a bullying policy
https://www.employment.govt.nz/tools-and-resources//SearchForm?Search=
bullying+policy
Bullying Prevention Toolkit
file:///C:/Users/info/Dropbox%20(Old)/My%20PC%20(DESKTOP-J6SR0LQ)/
Downloads/workplace-bullying-prevention-toolkit.pdf
Resolving sexual harassment
https://screensafe.co.nz/wp-content/uploads/2022/07/Sexual-Harassment-
Prevention-checklist.pdf
https://www.employment.govt.nz/resolving-problems/types-of-problems/
bullying-harassment-and-discrimination/sexual-harassment/what-is-sexual-
harassment/
Resolving discrimination
https://www.employment.govt.nz/resolving-problems/types-of-problems/bullying-
harassment-and-discrimination/discrimination-against-transgender-people/
Dealing with misconduct and serious misconduct
https://www.employment.govt.nz/resolving-problems/types-of-problems/
misconduct-and-serious-misconduct/
How to escalate unresolved problems
https://www.employment.govt.nz/resolving-problems/escalation-unresolved-
problems/

www.ingramcontent.com/pod-product-compliance
Lightning Source LLC
Chambersburg PA
CBHW070428010526
44118CB00014B/1953